HOW
DEMOCRACY
ENDS

HOW
DEMOCRACY
ENDS

David Runciman

BASIC BOOKS
New York

Basic Books
Hachette Book Group
1290 Avenue of the Americas, New York, NY 10104
www.basicbooks.com

Printed in the United States of America

First published in Great Britain by Profile Books Ltd in May 2018

First US Edition: June 2018

Published by Basic Books, an imprint of Perseus Books, LLC, a subsidiary of Hachette Book Group, Inc. The Basic Books name and logo is a trademark of the Hachette Book Group.

The Hachette Speakers Bureau provides a wide range of authors for speaking events. To find out more, go to www.hachettespeakers bureau.com or call (866) 376-6591.

The publisher is not responsible for websites (or their content) that are not owned by the publisher.

Library of Congress Cataloging-in-Publication Data has been applied for.

ISBNs: 978-1-5416-1678-3 (hardcover), 978-1-5416-1679-0 (e-book)

LSC-C

10 9 8 7 6 5 4 3 2 1

Contents

PREFACE

Thinking the unthinkable

NOTHING LASTS FOREVER. At some point democracy was always going to pass into the pages of history. No one, not even Francis Fukuyama – who announced the end of history back in 1989 – has believed that its virtues make it immortal.[1] But until very recently, most citizens of Western democracies would have imagined that the end was a long way off. They would not have expected it to happen in their lifetimes. Very few would have thought it might be taking place before their eyes.

Yet here we are, barely two decades into the twenty-first century, and almost from nowhere the question is upon us: is this how democracy ends?

Like many people, I first found myself confronting this question after the election of Donald Trump to the presidency of the United States. To borrow a phrase from philosophy, it looked like the *reductio ad absurdum* of democratic politics: any process that produces such a ridiculous conclusion must have gone seriously wrong somewhere along the way. If Trump is the answer, we are no longer asking the right question. But it's not just Trump. His election is symptomatic of an overheated political climate that appears increasingly unstable, riven with mistrust and mutual intolerance, fuelled by wild accusations and online bullying, a dialogue of the deaf drowning each other out with noise. In many places, not just the United States, democracy is starting to look unhinged.

Let me make it clear at the outset: I don't believe that Trump's arrival in the White House spells the end of democracy. America's democratic institutions are designed to withstand all kinds of bumps along the road and Trump's strange, erratic presidency is not outside the bounds of what can be survived. It is more likely that his administration will be followed by something relatively routine than by something even more outlandish. However, Trump's arrival in the White House poses a direct challenge: What would democratic failure in a country like the United States actually involve? What are the things that an established democracy could not survive? We now know we ought to start asking these questions. But we don't know how to answer them.

Our political imaginations are stuck with outdated images of what democratic failure looks like. We are trapped in the landscape of the twentieth century. We reach back to the 1930s or to the 1970s for pictures of what happens when democracy falls apart: tanks in the streets; tin-pot dictators barking out messages of national unity, violence and repression in tow. Trump's presidency has drawn widespread comparison with tyrannies of the past. We have been warned not to be complacent in thinking it couldn't happen again. But what of the other danger: that while we are looking out for the familiar signs of failure, our democracies are going wrong in ways with which we are unfamiliar? This strikes me as the greater threat. I do not think there is much chance that we are going back to the 1930s. We are not at a second pre-dawn of fascism, violence and world war. Our societies are too different – too affluent, too elderly, too networked – and our collective historical knowledge of what went wrong then is too entrenched. When democracy ends, we are likely to be surprised by the form it takes. We may not even notice that it is happening because we are looking in the wrong places.

Contemporary political science has little to say about new ways that democracy might fail because it is preoccupied with a different question: how democracy gets going in the first place. This is understandable. During the period that democracy has spread around the world the process has often been two steps forward, one step back. Democracy might get tentatively established in parts of Africa or Latin America or Asia and then a coup or military takeover would snuff it out, before someone tried again. This has happened in places from Chile to South Korea to Kenya. One of the central puzzles of political science is what causes democracy to stick. It is fundamentally a question of trust: people with something to lose from the results of an election have to believe it is worth persevering until the next time. The rich need to trust that the poor won't take their money. The soldiers need to trust that the civilians won't take their guns. Often, that trust breaks down. Then democracy falls apart.

As a result, political scientists tend to think of democratic failure in terms of what they call 'backsliding'. A democracy reverts back to the point before lasting confidence in its institutions could be established. This is why we look for earlier examples of democratic failure to illuminate what might go wrong in the present. We assume that the end of democracy takes us back to the beginning. The process of creation goes into reverse.

In this book I want to offer a different perspective. What would political failure look like in societies where confidence in democracy is so firmly established that it is hard to shake? The question for the twenty-first century is how long we can persist with institutional arrangements we have grown so used to trusting, that we no longer notice when they have ceased to work. These arrangements include regular elections, which remain the bedrock of democratic politics. But they also encompass democratic legislatures, independent law courts and a free press. All can continue to function as they ought while failing to deliver what they should. A hollowed-out version of democracy risks lulling us into a false sense of security. We might continue to trust in it and to look to it for rescue, even as we seethe with irritation at its inability to answer the call. Democracy could fail while remaining intact.

This analysis might seem at odds with the frequent talk about the loss of trust in democratic politics and politicians across Western societies. It is true that many voters dislike and distrust their elected representatives now more than ever. But it is not the kind of loss of trust that leads people to take up arms against democracy. Instead, it is the kind that leads them to throw up their arms in despair. Democracy can survive that sort of behaviour for a long time. Where it ends up is an open question and one I will try to answer. But it does not end up in the 1930s.

We should try to avoid the Benjamin Button view of history, which imagines that old things become young again, even as they acquire more experience. History does not go into reverse. It is true that contemporary Western democracy is behaving in ways that seem to echo some of the darkest moments in our past – anyone who watched protestors with swastikas demonstrating on the streets of Charlottesville, Virginia, and then heard the president of the United States managing to find fault on both sides, could be forgiven for fearing the worst. However, grim though these events are, they are not the precursors of a return to something we thought we'd left behind. We really have left the twentieth century behind. We need another frame of reference.

So let me offer a different analogy. It is not perfect, but I hope it helps make sense of the argument of this book. Western democracy is going through a mid-life crisis. That is not to trivialise what's happening: mid-life crises can be disastrous and even fatal. And this is a full-blown crisis. But it needs to be understood in relation to the exhaustion of democracy as well as to its volatility, and to the complacency that is currently on display as well as to the anger. The symptoms of a mid-life crisis include behaviour we might associate with someone much younger. But it would be a mistake to assume that the way to understand what's going on is to study how young people behave.

When a miserable middle-aged man buys a motorbike on impulse, it can be dangerous. If he is really unlucky it all ends in a fireball. But it is nothing like as dangerous as when a seventeen-year-old buys a motorbike. More often, it is simply embarrassing. The mid-life motorbike gets ridden a few times and ends up parked in the street. Maybe it gets sold. The crisis will need to be resolved in some other way, if it can be resolved at all. American democracy is in miserable middle age. Donald Trump is its motorbike. It could still end in a fireball. More likely, the crisis will continue and it will need to be resolved in some other way, if it can be resolved at all.

I am conscious that talking about the crisis of democracy in these terms might sound self-indulgent, especially coming from a privileged, middle-aged white man. Acting out like this is a luxury many people around the world cannot afford. These are first world problems. The crisis is real but it is also a bit of a joke. That's what makes it so hard to know how it might end.

To suffer a crisis that comes neither at the beginning nor at the end but somewhere in the middle of a life is to be pulled forwards and backwards at the same time. What pulls us forwards is our wish for something better. What pulls us back is our reluctance to let go of something that has got us this far. The reluctance is understandable: democracy has served us well. The appeal of modern democracy lies in its ability to deliver long-term benefits for societies while providing their individual citizens with a voice. This is a formidable combination. It is easy to see why we don't want to give up on it, at least not yet. However, the choice might not simply be between the whole democratic package and some alternative, anti-democratic package. It may be that the elements that make democracy so attractive continue to operate but that they no longer work together. The package starts to come apart. When an individual starts to unravel, we sometimes say that he or she is in pieces. At present democracy looks like it is in pieces. That does not mean it is unmendable. Not yet.

So what are the factors that make the current crisis in democracy unlike those it has faced in the past, when it was younger? I believe there are three fundamental differences. First, political violence is not what it was for earlier generations, either in scale or in character. Western democracies are fundamentally peaceful societies, which means that our most destructive impulses manifest themselves in other ways. There is still violence, of course. But it stalks the fringes of our politics and the recesses of our imaginations, without ever arriving centre stage. It is the ghost in this story. Second, the threat of catastrophe has changed. Where the prospect of disaster once had a galvanising effect, now it tends to be stultifying. We freeze in the face of our fears. Third, the information technology revolution has completely altered the terms on which democracy must operate. We have become dependent on forms of communication and information-sharing that we neither control nor fully understand. All of these features of our democracy are consistent with its getting older.

I have organised this book around these three themes: coup; catastrophe; technological takeover. I start with coups – the standard markers of democratic failure – to ask whether an armed takeover of democratic institutions is still a realistic possibility. If not, how could democracy be subverted without the use of force being required? Would we even know it was happening? The spread of conspiracy theories is a symptom of our growing uncertainty about where the threat really lies. Coups require conspiracies because they need to be plotted by small groups in secret, or else they don't work. Without them, we are just left with the conspiracy theories, which settle nothing.

Next I explore the risk of catastrophe. Democracy will fail if everything else falls apart: nuclear war, calamitous climate change, bio-terrorism, the rise of the killer robots could all finish off democratic politics, though that would be the least of our worries. If something goes truly, terribly wrong, the people who are left will be too busy scrabbling for survival to care much about voting for change. But how big is the risk that, if confronted with these threats, the life drains out of democracy anyway, as we find ourselves paralysed by indecision?

Then I discuss the possibility of technological takeover. Intelligent robots are still some way off. But low-level, semi-intelligent machines that mine data for us and stealthily take the decisions we are too busy to make are gradually infiltrating much of our lives. We now have technology that promises greater efficiency than anything we've ever seen before, controlled by corporations that are less accountable than any in modern political history. Will we abdicate democratic responsibility to these new forces without even saying goodbye?

Finally, I ask whether it makes sense to look to replace democracy with something better. A mid-life crisis can be a sign that we really do need to change. If we are stuck in a rut, why don't we make a clean break from what's making us so miserable? Churchill famously called democracy the worst system of government apart from all the others that have been tried from time to time. He said it back in 1947. That was a long time ago. Has there really been nothing better to try since then? I review some of the alternatives, from twenty-first century authoritarianism to twenty-first century anarchism.

To conclude, I consider how the story of democracy might actually wind up. In my view, it will not have a single endpoint. Given their very different life experiences, democracies will continue to follow different paths in different parts of the world. Just because American democracy can survive Trump doesn't mean that Turkish democracy can survive Erdogan. Democracy could thrive in Africa even as it starts to fail in parts of Europe. What happens to democracy in the West is not necessarily going to determine the fate of democracy everywhere. But Western democracy is still the flagship model for democratic progress. Its failure would have enormous implications for the future of politics.

Whatever happens – unless the end of the world comes first – this will be a drawn-out demise. The current American experience of democracy is at the heart of the story that I tell, but it needs to be understood against the wider experience of democracy in other times and other places. In arguing that we ought to get away from our current fixation with the 1930s, I am not suggesting that history is unimportant. Quite the opposite: our obsession with a few traumatic moments in our past can blind us to the many lessons to be drawn from other points in time. For there is as much to learn from the 1890s as from the 1930s. I go further back: to the 1650s and to the democracy of the ancient world. We need history to help us break free from our unhealthy fixations with our own immediate back story. It is therapy for the middle-aged.

The future will be different from the past. The past is longer than we think. America is not the whole world. Nevertheless, the immediate American past is where I begin, with the inauguration of President Trump. That was not the moment at which democracy came to an end. But it was a good moment to start thinking about what the end of democracy might mean.

INTRODUCTION ·

20 January 2017

I WATCHED THE INAUGURATION of Donald Trump as president of the United States on a large screen in a lecture hall in Cambridge, England. The room was full of international students, wrapped up against the cold – public rooms in Cambridge are not always well heated and there were as many people in coats and scarves inside the hall as there were on the podium in Washington, DC. But the atmosphere among the students was not chilly. Many were laughing and joking. The mood felt quite festive, like at any public funeral.

When Trump began to speak, the laughing soon stopped. Up on the big screen, against a backdrop of pillars and draped American flags, he looked forbidding and strange. We were scared. Trump's barking delivery and his crudely effective hand gestures – slicing the thin air with his stubby fingers, raising a clenched fist at the climax of his address – had many of us thinking the same thing: this is what the cartoon version of fascism looks like. The resemblance to a scene in a Batman movie – the Joker addressing the cowed citizens of Gotham – was so strong it seemed like a cliché. That doesn't make it the wrong analogy. Clichés are where the truth goes to die.

The speech Trump gave was shocking. He used

apocalyptic turns of phrase that echoed the wild, angry fringes of democratic politics where democracy can start to turn into its opposite. He bemoaned 'the rusted-out factories scattered like tombstones across the landscape of our nation … the crime and gangs and drugs'. In calling for a rebirth of national pride, he reminded his audience that 'we all bleed the same red blood of patriots'. It sounded like a thinly veiled threat. Above all, he cast doubt on the basic idea of representative government, which is that the citizens entrust elected politicians to take decisions on their behalf. Trump lambasted professional politicians for having betrayed the American people and forfeited their trust:

> For too long, a small group in our nation's capital has reaped the rewards of government while the people have borne the cost.
>
> Washington flourished – but the people did not share its wealth.
>
> Politicians prospered – but the jobs left, and the factories closed.[2]

He insisted that his election marked the moment when power passed not just from president to president or from party to party, but from Washington, DC back to the people. Was he going to mobilise popular anger against any professionals who now stood in his way? Who would be able to stop him? When he had finished speaking, he was greeted in our lecture hall back in Cambridge by a stunned silence. We weren't the only ones taken aback. Trump's predecessor but one in the presidency, George W. Bush, was heard to mutter as he left the stage: 'That was some weird shit.'

Then, because we live in an age when everything that's been consumed can be instantly re-consumed, we decided to watch it again. Second time around was different. I found the speech less shocking, once I knew what was coming. I felt that I had overreacted. Just because Trump said all these things didn't make them true. His fearsome talk was at odds with the basic civility of the scene. Wouldn't a country that was as fractured as he said have found it hard to sit politely through his inauguration? It was also at odds with what I knew about America. It is not a broken society, certainly not by any historical standards.

Notwithstanding some recent blips, violence is in overall decline. Prosperity is rising, though it remains very unequally distributed. If people had really believed what Trump said, would they have voted for him? That would have been a very brave act, given the risks of total civil breakdown. Maybe they voted for him because they didn't really believe him?

It took me about fifteen minutes to acclimatise to the idea that this rhetoric was the new normal. Trump's speechwriters, Steve Bannon and Stephen Miller, had put no words in his mouth that were explicitly anti-democratic. It was a populist speech, but populism does not oppose democracy. Rather, it tries to reclaim it from the elites who have betrayed it. Nothing Trump said disputed the fundamental premise of representative democracy, which is that at the allotted time the people get to say when they have had enough of the politicians who have been making decisions for them. Trump was echoing what those who voted for him clearly believed: enough was enough.

Watching the speech over again, I found myself focusing less on Trump and more on the people arrayed alongside him. Melania Trump looked alarmed to be on the stage with her husband. President Obama merely looked uncomfortable. Hillary Clinton, off to the side, looked dazed. The joint chiefs were stony-faced and stoical. The truth is that there is little Trump could have said after taking the oath of office that would have posed a direct threat to American democracy. These were just words. What matters in politics is when words become deeds. The only people with the power to end American democracy on 20 January 2017 were the ones sitting beside him. And they were doing nothing.

How might it have been different? The minimal definition of democracy says simply that the losers of an election accept that they have lost. They hand over power without resort to violence. In other words, they grin and bear it. If that happens once, you have the makings of a democracy. If it happens twice, you have a democracy that's built to last. In America, it has happened fifty-seven times that the losers in a presidential election have accepted the result, though occasionally it has been touch and go (notably in the much-disputed 1876 election and in 2000, when the loser of the popular vote, as with Trump, went on to win the presidency). On twenty-one occasions the US has seen a peaceful transfer of power from one party to another. Only once, in 1861, has American democracy failed this test – when a group of Southern states could not endure the idea of Abraham Lincoln as their legitimate president, and fought against it for four years.

To put it another way: democracy is civil war without the fighting.[3] Failure comes when proxy battles turn into real ones. The biggest single danger to American democracy following Trump's victory was if either President Obama or Hillary Clinton had refused to accept the result. Clinton won the popular vote by a large margin – 2.9 million votes, more than any defeated candidate in US history – and she ended up the loser thanks to the archaic rules of the Electoral College.

On the night of the election, Clinton was having difficulty accepting that she had been beaten, as defeated candidates often do. Obama called her to insist that she acknowledge the outcome as soon as possible. The future of American democracy depended on it.

In that respect, a more significant speech than Trump's inaugural was the one Obama gave on the lawn of the White House on 9 November, the day after the election. He had arrived to find many of his staffers in tears, aghast at the thought that eight years of hard work were about to be undone by a man who seemed completely unqualified for the office to which he had been elected. It was only hours after the result had been declared and angry Democrats were already questioning Trump's legitimacy. Obama took the opposite tack:

> You know, the path this country has taken has never been a straight line. We zig and zag and sometimes we move in ways that some people think is forwards and others think is moving back and that's OK …
> The point is that we all go forward with a presumption of good faith in our fellow citizens because that presumption of good faith is essential to a vibrant and functioning democracy … And that's why I'm confident that this incredible journey that we're on as Americans will go on. And I'm looking forward to doing everything I can to make sure the next president is successful in that.[4]

It is easy to see why Obama felt he had no choice except to say what he did. Anything else would have thrown the workings of democracy into doubt. But it is worth asking: What are the circumstances in which a sitting president might feel compelled to say something different? When does faith in the zig and zag of democratic politics stop being a precondition of progress and start to become a hostage to fortune?

Had Clinton won the 2016 election – especially if she had somehow contrived to win the Electoral College while losing the popular vote – it is unlikely Trump would have been so magnanimous. He made it clear throughout the campaign that his willingness to accept the result depended on whether or not he was the winner. A defeated Trump could well have challenged the core premise of democratic politics that, as Obama put it, 'if we lose, we learn from our mistakes, we do some reflection, we lick our wounds, we brush ourselves off, we get back in the arena'.[5] Licking his wounds is not Trump's style. If the worst-case scenario for a democracy is an election in which the two sides disagree about whether the result holds, then American democracy dodged a bullet in 2016.

It is easy to imagine that Trump might have chosen to boycott the inauguration of Hillary Clinton, had he lost. That scenario would have been ugly, and petty, and it could have turned violent, but it need not have been fatal to constitutional government. The republic could have muddled through. On the other hand, had Obama refused to permit Trump's inauguration, on the grounds that he was still occupying the White House, or that he was planning to install Clinton there, then democracy in America would have been done for, at least for now.

There is another shorthand for the minimal definition of a functioning democracy: the people with guns don't use them. Trump's supporters have plenty of guns and, had he lost, some of these people might have been tempted to use them. Nevertheless, there is a big difference between an opposition candidate refusing to accept defeat and an incumbent refusing to leave office. No matter how much firepower the supporters of the aggrieved loser might have at their disposal, the state always has more. If it doesn't, it is no longer a functioning state. The 'people with guns' in the minimal definition of democracy refers to the politicians who control the armed forces. Democracy fails when elected officials who have the authority to tell the generals what to do refuse to give it up. Or when the generals refuse to listen.

This means that the other players who had the capacity to deal democracy a fatal blow on 20 January were also sitting beside Trump: America's military chiefs. If they had declined to accept the orders of their new commander-in-chief – for instance, if they had decided he could not be trusted with the nuclear codes – then no amount of ceremony would have hidden the fact that the inauguration was an empty charade. One reason for the air of mild hilarity in our lecture hall in Cambridge was that the rumour quickly passed around that Trump had been in possession of the nuclear football since breakfast time. The joke was that we were lucky still to be here. But none of us would have been smiling if the joint chiefs had decided that the new president was best kept in the dark. Even more alarming than an erratic new president in possession of the power to unleash destruction is the prospect of the generals deciding to keep that power for themselves.

Yet it is worth asking the same questions of the generals as of the sitting president: When is it appropriate to refuse to obey the orders of a duly elected commander-in-chief? Trump came into office surrounded by rumours that he was under the influence of a foreign power. He was certainly inexperienced, likely irresponsible and possibly compromised. American democracy has survived worse – if inexperience and irresponsibility in international affairs were a barrier to the highest office, then the history of the presidency would be very different. It is the knowledge that American democracy has survived worse that makes it so hard to know how to respond now. In Cambridge, we laughed for a bit, and then we sat in glum silence. In Washington, they did the same.

Trump's inauguration allows us to sketch out three different versions of how a democracy like the United States could fail. The first is more or less unthinkable: Trump wins by the rules, and the American state refuses to recognise his victory. He is denied the keys to the White House by the sitting president and the military reject his authority. That is the route to civil war. Obama ruled it out of bounds almost the moment the result was known. The second is something that could have happened but didn't: Hillary wins and Donald refuses to recognise her victory. Civil war does not necessarily follow. It all depends on how much violence Trump's disappointed supporters are willing both to inflict and to endure. We will never know the answer to that question. My guess is that, for all the angry words, sustained violence was never likely. Some people might be prepared to kill for Trump. But to die for him? That's something else again.

The third scenario is the one that actually happened: Trump wins and the American political establishment decides to grin and bear it. Some reluctantly clamber aboard his administration in the hope of providing a steadying influence. Others grimace and wait for the worst to pass. They believe that Trump's words can be absorbed and tamed by the flexibility of America's democratic institutions. It is a gamble – what if Trump cannot be tamed? – but it is not a reckless one. The alternative – refusing to accept Trump as president – looks far more reckless. It is not the same gamble as the catastrophic one taken by the German political establishment in 1932–3, when politicians who thought they could tame Hitler ended up consumed by him instead. Twenty-first century America is nothing like Weimar Germany. Its democratic institutions are much more battle-hardened. Its society is much more prosperous. Its population has many better things to do than take up arms against democracy.

As I write, the bet is not yet settled. But the odds still look favourable for the survival of democracy. It is possible to argue that since Trump was elected, American democracy has been working as it is meant to. There has been an ongoing contest between Trump's disruptive menace and a system designed to withstand a lot of disruption, especially when it emanates from demagoguery. The demagogue is discovering the world of difference between words and deeds. He is ensnared by institutions that have pushed back against his demands for personal loyalty.

Congress has not proved as biddable as he might have hoped. The courts have also provided a barrier to executive action. Where vacancies arise, Trump has been relatively successful in filling them with judges sympathetic to his cause, such as it is. This contrasts with his inability, or unwillingness, to re-populate the bureaucracy of the federal government, where many posts remain vacant. Yet there are too many courts and too many judges for such a strategy to be decisive in the short term. As with any American president, the effects of his impact on the judiciary are only likely to be felt long after he is gone. Any populist revolt that seeks to rely on the courts to get things done is likely to be a pretty muted uprising. Trump has his acolytes and his fellow travellers, but so do all presidents. Beyond his narrow circle, which is shrinking all the time, the institutions of American democracy are proving relatively resistant to capture.

For Trump's committed supporters, however, this outcome is not so different from the first scenario. They argue that the American state did not deny him power by refusing to recognise his victory because it did not need to do anything so explicit. Instead, the 'deep state' set out to undermine Trump's presidency from his first day in office. The betrayal is all happening behind the scenes. On this account, democracy ceased to work a long time ago, because no president who set out to challenge the authority of the political establishment would be allowed to get away with it. There has been no coup against Trump. Yet talk of a coup has been incessant since the moment he took office, with his supporters accusing his enemies in his own party as well as the liberal establishment of organising a plot to bring him to heel. The conservative political commentator and rabble-rouser Rush Limbaugh calls this 'the silent coup'.[6] It is almost as though no one knows what a coup means any more.

For Trump's diehard opponents, by contrast, we are living through a warped variant of scenario two. Although Trump won, he never acknowledged the consequence of his own victory: that he was meant to start behaving like a president. He refused even to recognise that he had lost the popular vote, claiming that it had been stolen from him by voter fraud. For the first time in history, the winner would not accept the result of a presidential election. Political science has little to say about that because it does not fit with any known theory of democracy. President Trump brooks no criticism and there is no fact he will not dispute if it suits him. It began with his inauguration, when he let it be known that the crowds in attendance were huge, despite all evidence to the contrary. He governs from outside the bounds of democratic civility, which requires recognition that there can be truth on the other side. He is making a mockery of the system that is tolerating him.

So while Trump is locked in a battle with America's democratic institutions, there is another contest going on among the people who refuse to accept that this is the real story. Theirs is the shadow world of conspiracy theories and alternative facts. It rests on the assumption that the true picture of what is happening can only be understood by imputing anti-democratic motives to the leading actors. Democracy may look like it's working, but it isn't really, because the other side is no longer playing by the rules. Under the terms of this mutually intolerant form of partisanship, political order has already broken down but no one is admitting it yet. Instead of civil war without the fighting, we have the verbal jousting without the civil war.

The existence of this netherworld of partisan conflict makes it hard to know how much trouble American democracy is in. If there had been empty chairs on the platform on the day of Trump's inauguration – or indeed no ceremony at all – then the threat to democracy would have been visible for all to see. The battle lines would have been drawn such that no one could dispute them. The same would be true if the event had broken down in violence, as some feared it might. We would know where we stood. But nothing happened that day to signal that the game was up. The affront to democracy was cartoonish. Everything else took place as it should, according to the rules of the game. The protests were angry but respectful. The dignitaries just about kept their dignity. If something is fundamentally amiss with American democracy, it is hiding in plain sight.

Like many people, I have spent much of the time since Trump's inauguration thinking about Trump.

Perhaps that is a mistake. America may not be the right place to anticipate the end of democracy, however much its current president commands our attention. The world watched transfixed on 20 January 2017 because it was so hard to look away. The theatre of Trump's presidency is compelling and it is absurd. Less compelling and potentially less absurd versions of the same drama are playing out elsewhere. The battle lines may be drawn more clearly in countries where elections are won by anti-establishment politicians from the left rather than from the right, or where democratic institutions are less entrenched or more easily co-opted. If the demise of democracy ultimately requires a full-blown military–civilian showdown, or an overt authoritarian takeover, then there are many places where it is more likely to happen than the United States. This book will therefore not just be about America: we will also look at Delhi and Istanbul, Athens and Budapest. Trump's presidency could be a vast distraction from the greater threats posed to democracy elsewhere.

But America still matters. What if the distraction is the real story? I don't mean this as a conspiracy theorist might. I am not suggesting that Trump's clownish antics are a deliberate attempt to throw people off the scent of a more concerted assault on democratic institutions. I still believe that with Trump what you see is what you get. The problem is that what you see is so hard to fathom. He is both ludicrous and threatening, familiar and peculiar, inside and outside the bounds of what a democracy can tolerate. My confused reaction to his inauguration – shock followed by the absence of shock, all in the space of fifteen minutes – was not a one-off. That is still how it feels. Trump, more than any other democratic politician in recent history, is capable of evoking contradictory emotions at the same time. He is ridiculous and he is deadly serious. He is incomprehensible and he is as open as a child. He is a reason to panic and he is a reason to keep calm and carry on.

Trump matters because of where he comes in the history of American democracy: not at the end, but somewhere in the middle, which may yet turn out to be the beginning of the end. The US is not just the world's most important democracy; it is also one of the oldest. It is an open question when to date the start of democracy in America. Some of it begins at the beginning, with the founding of the republic in 1776. But no republic founded on slavery can be a true democracy in the modern sense. Even with slavery abolished, many citizens were still disenfranchised. It was only in the twentieth century, with the enfranchisement of women and later the civil rights movement, that something close to what we now think of as democracy finally arrived. That makes current American democracy no more than one hundred years old, and perhaps no more than fifty or sixty. By political standards, that is not elderly. It is not youthful either, given how many democracies have been snuffed out before they have even got going. It is middle-aged. Ancient Athenian democracy lived to be two hundred before it expired. By that measure, democracy in America is not even halfway done.

It is never easy to think about death – least of all one's own death. But when you are middle-aged it is time to start. You know it is coming – it is no longer possible to believe, as when one is young, that mortality is something that only happens to other people. To be middle-aged is to have survived long enough to recognise the signs. Dramatic collapse is possible – it's happened to others. At the same time, treating every ache and pain as a signal that the end is at hand is laughable. Hypochondria is a malady in itself. Life is still to be lived and the best may yet be to come. That's where American democracy is now.

The history of political thought is littered with comparisons between the artificial lives of states and the natural condition of human beings. These analogies are often bogus and disreputable. Reflecting on the mortality of the body politic can simply be an excuse to argue for continuity at all costs. 'The king is dead! Long live the king!' But there is still something for politics to learn from how people grow old. Democracy in America has reached a tired and crotchety middle age. It is not immune from hypochondria. Fearing death from the slightest cause is not the same as thinking seriously about death. It makes concerted action more difficult because it can breed a sense of helplessness. It can also breed the sort of recklessness that comes with feeling you have little left to lose. There are many different ways to experience a mid-life crisis. America may now be going through a number of them all at once.

The glaring flaw in any analogy between the lifespan of political regimes and those of human beings is that we know roughly how long humans can live for. Or at least we think we do. With states we really have no idea. Just because Athenian democracy died at two hundred doesn't mean that's the natural condition of democracy. Even if American democracy is somewhere in the middle of its existence, we lack any reliable way of knowing whether it is nearer the beginning or the end.

At the same time, doubts are starting to grow about the human side of this equation. In a few places, including Silicon Valley, a tiny number of privileged human beings are starting to contemplate the possibility of their own immortality. Technological advances mean that the first individuals to buck a natural life span – whether by extending their lives for two hundred years, or two thousand, or for ever – may already be alive. Perhaps American democracy is soon going to look more mortal than some of the people who inhabit it. The need to keep the state alive was always premised on the idea that it could outlive its citizens: that's what gave them the imperative to die for it when called upon. What if it is called upon to die for them? The logic of longevity may be changing.

The inauguration of Donald Trump saw an old man with the political personality of a child come to the head of a state in uncomfortable middle age at a point when human mortality is no longer an absolute given. It is time to think again about what it means for democracy to live and die.

We will return to Washington. But first, we need to go back to Athens.

1

Coup!

WHEN A DEMOCRACY fails, we usually expect the failure to be spectacular. It is a public event, familiar enough in modern history to have acquired a ceremony of its own. Democracy has died many times round the world. We know what it looks like. It looks something like this:

Nothing was announced in advance. Tanks surrounded the city overnight and soldiers were sent to seize key communications points, including the radio and television stations and the post office. The prime minister was arrested. So was the man who had been expected to succeed him in elections due to be held in three weeks' time. Parliament and the royal palace were occupied. The soldiers circulated lists of dangerous individuals, who were rounded up and kept in isolation. All this happened in the space of a few hours. The colonels leading the coup went to visit the king at his weekend residence to demand that he confirm them as the legitimate new rulers of the nation. They told him: 'The coup was done in your name to save the country.' When the furious king demanded, 'Where is my prime minister? Where is my government?' he was told, 'You have none. We have arrested them all.'[7]

The city was Athens, on the night of 21 April 1967. The primary target of the coup was Andreas Papandreou, leader of the leftist group within his father Georgios Papandreou's Centre Union, which had been confidently expected to form the next democratically elected government of Greece. Elements of the armed forces, egged on by American intelligence, suspected the younger Papandreou was planning to take Greece out of NATO. They also believed he would attempt a purge of their own ranks. Following a rooftop chase, Andreas Papandreou was captured at bayonet point in his country villa and taken to a small hotel, where he was held under heavy armed guard. He was visited there by the *New York Times* journalist Cyrus Sulzberger, who reported: 'He put on a gallant front but he looked a tiny bit grey around the mouth and couldn't keep his hands still, the way it sometimes happens when people are frightened.'[8] Papandreou didn't know that King Constantine had made it a condition of accepting the colonels' demands that no one be shot out of hand. For twenty-four hours the future prime minister couldn't be sure if he would live or die.

The coup succeeded because it was quick, decisive and took its victims by surprise. This included the head of the armed forces, who did not know what his junior officers were planning. The people of Greece went to bed one night believing they were living in a democracy and woke up next day to find that this was no longer true. It is the hallmark of a successful coup d'état that there is a before and an after, marked by a series of events that signal the unequivocal difference between them. On 22 April, Greek radio suspended normal broadcasting to play martial music, interrupted by announcements of the decrees of the new regime: political parties were to be abolished, military courts established and freedom of speech suspended. Meanwhile, the tanks remained on the streets. The point of a coup like this is that no one should be in any doubt about what has happened, because the absence of doubt is the only way to secure obedience. The alternatives are failure or civil war.

The speed with which the end came does not mean that a healthy democracy got snuffed out in an instant, as when a fit person drops dead from a heart attack. Greek democracy had been in a bad way for a long time. The causes of the coup are still widely debated because there are so many to choose from. The country was divided ideologically between left and right and institutionally between king, army and parliament. None of the different factions trusted each other and there were cabals within cabals. Elections did not settle their differences: the one held in 1961 was widely seen as having been stolen by the winners – the right-wing National Radical Union (ERE) – after a campaign marked by violence. A number of leading politicians had been murdered, yet the perpetrators were rarely brought to justice. Prime ministers came and went, appointed by the king without parliamentary backing. It was hard to say who was in charge. Perhaps no one was.

Meanwhile, Greece was on the front line in the Cold War, which made the stakes far higher than if this had just been a little local difficulty. For those who had eyes to see, CIA involvement could be detected everywhere. Sulzberger was assumed to be a CIA agent – how else did he get access to the imprisoned Papandreou so quickly? On the other hand, if it wasn't the Americans, it was the Russians. Moderate leftists were accused of being secret communists. Paranoia was rife and conspiracy theories flourished, fuelled by the age-old fear of a Turkish invasion. During the Cold War being paranoid made a lot of sense, especially for states like Greece that found themselves pawns in the geopolitical power play. Greece was a poor country by European standards and barely twenty years out of a full-blown civil war. Its democracy had been built on very shaky foundations. The coup, when it came, was both a surprise and an event long foretold.

The weakness of Greek democracy explains how a coup was possible. It also explains why, to its perpetrators, a coup was necessary. The colonels were exploiting the political divisions that in their own minds gave them the justification for taking matters into their own hands. Because democracy was not working, it had to be terminated. Yet that is the problem with justifying a coup: the explanation is never fully convincing. If democracy is so weak and ineffectual, why is such brutal action needed to end it? Why all the arrests, the tanks in the streets, the martial music? What were the colonels afraid of, if not of democracy itself?

Now fast-forward fifty years. Greek democracy is in deep trouble once again. The country continues to be split by profound ideological and institutional divisions. The economic situation is dire: Greece has undergone one of the worst depressions of modern times. The fall in national income has been longer, deeper and more dramatic than America endured during the Great Depression. Youth unemployment stands at above 50 per cent. Conspiracy theories are rife, with the Germans now attracting much of the blame for what's gone wrong. They are seen as the powers behind the throne, even though there is no throne any more. Elections don't seem to help: no matter who wins, the same problems persist. Trust in democratic politics is at an all-time low.

These are conditions that look ripe for another coup. Greece still has a relatively well-funded army – the age-old fear of a Turkish invasion has never gone away. Add to the mix angry citizens, divided elites, deep economic distress and interfering foreign powers and all the ingredients are here for democracy come to an end. Yet there has been no military coup in Greece since the fall of the colonels in 1974 and it seems very unlikely there will be another one. The Greek parliament does contain a neo-fascist party, Golden Dawn, that openly expresses its admiration for military dictatorship. This remains a minority view: the party rarely polls above 10 per cent. The realistic prospect of a military takeover is remote. If Greece were to undergo a repeat of 1967 it would not just be a shock. It would be almost inexplicable.

What has changed? First, the institutional divisions now run along completely different lines. In place of king, army and parliament, the current impasse is between the European Union (EU), the banks and parliament. No one is coming to this contest with guns already in their pockets. The battles are taking place between men and women in business suits armed with spreadsheets. The Greek army is not an active participant in this power struggle. It is simply a bystander.

Second, the Cold War is over. This is no longer an existential struggle between Western democracy and its ideological enemies. Greece is on the frontline of a different showdown, between international finance and national sovereignty. It is struggling to cope with an influx of refugees from civil wars elsewhere, including in Syria. The United States has an interest in what happens to Greece, but it does not see its own survival at stake, as it did when it feared a communist takeover. The CIA has got other fish to fry. The bright lines of the Cold War have given way to the murk of suspected Russian interference in domestic politics, which can be seen everywhere and nowhere. The Chinese are involved as well, but they have no desire to militarise the situation. Rather, they are looking for investment opportunities.

If the political circumstances have changed, so has Greece itself. It is a very different country than it was in 1967. It is much poorer than it was ten years ago, after a decade in which GDP has fallen by around a quarter. But it is still much, much richer than it was fifty years ago. The Greek economy grew five-fold between 1968 and 2008, with per capita GDP reaching a peak of around $30,000. The figure is now nearer $20,000. That still places Greece well above the threshold that political scientists have identified as the point where democratic societies are vulnerable to a military takeover. No democracy has reverted to military rule once GDP is greater than $8,000 per person. Why? It is hard to say for sure. But it seems likely that greater wealth changes the incentive structure for those involved. When everyone has more to lose – soldiers and politicians, as well as citizens – they think twice before tearing the whole thing down.

Greece is a much more elderly society than it was fifty years ago. It currently has one of the highest median ages in the world: half the population is aged 46 or older. There has been relatively little violence in Greece during the current crisis, certainly compared to the bloodshed of the 1960s and 1970s. Political violence is a young man's game. One reason its high youth unemployment has not proved more destabilising is that there simply aren't that many young people in Greece any more. There are far more pensioners than there are students. In demographic terms, the situation is starting to look terminal: in some Greek villages only one person is being born for every ten who die. Nearly half a million Greeks have left the country since the economic crisis began in 2008, around 5 per cent of the total population. Many people under 40 are still living at home, surviving off what's left of their parents' and grandparents' income. A slow demographic death may be one of the things that help to keep democracy alive. Entropy replaces explosive change as the default condition of politics.

Old people also have memories that young people lack. Golden Dawn gets much of its support from alienated younger Greeks. They are not so bothered by the party's ties to the era of the colonels because they have no memory and little knowledge of it. But older Greeks remember what it was like. It was a time of violence and oppression. It ended in failure, to be replaced by a form of politics that brought peace and prosperity. Anyone who has lived through the last fifty years of Greek history will be loath to give up on democracy just yet. It may be struggling to deal with the current crisis. But compared to what preceded it, democracy still looks like a decent bet.

There is another possibility, however. As well as Greece having changed and its political situation having changed, it may be that coups have also changed.

The Greek finance minister Yanis Varoufakis spent much of his time in office during 2015 worrying about the imminence of a coup. He describes his fears in *Adults in the Room*, his 2017 memoir of that knife-edge period. Varoufakis is not an impartial witness. His tenure in the Syriza government was brief – it ran for just six months at the height of the crisis over a potential Greek default on its massive sovereign debt. As finance minister, Varoufakis pursued a strategy that challenged Greece's creditors – including the International Monetary Fund (IMF) and the member states of the EU, above all Germany – to restructure Greek debt or face the potentially catastrophic consequences of Greece leaving the Eurozone. It was a high-risk approach, given that Greece had few weapons at its disposal that would not inflict massive self-harm. By contrast, the arsenal on the other side was formidable. The Greek economy was on life support, propped up by a series of temporary loans from the European Central Bank (ECB). If Varoufakis pushed his opponents too far, they had the option of pulling the plug on the Greek banking system. For each day of his time in office, Varoufakis lived in dread of waking up to find that the banks had shut.

This is what he means by a coup. It does not involve tanks or soldiers or arrests. It simply requires that a democratically elected government be held to ransom by forces it lacks the power to resist. It had already happened to one of Greece's near neighbours.

> [In 2013] a new government had just been elected in Cyprus. The following day the troika [the representatives of the IMF, the EC and the ECB] closed down the island's banks, dictating terms to the new president for their re-opening. Incredulous but unprepared, the new president had signed on the dotted line. [9]

This was the equivalent of what the colonels had done to the king in 1967, only without anyone having to use armed force. Varoufakis calls it a 'dress rehearsal' for what the troika intended to do to Greece. He also calls it 'the Cyprus coup'.

At only one point did Varoufakis consider the possibility of the other kind of coup, involving people with actual guns. It came on the night he resigned from the government, following the July 2015 referendum when the Greek people had voted overwhelmingly to reject the troika's latest demands. Varoufakis confronted the prime minister, Alexis Tsipras, to insist that they act on the people's wishes and prepare to stand up to their creditors. Tsipras replied that they could not follow through. If they did, he insinuated, 'then something like a coup might take place ... the president of the republic, the intelligence services were in a "readied state"'. [10] Varoufakis was unmoved. 'Let them do their worst!' was his defiant response.

A coup that overturned the result of the referendum would have had the advantage of signalling that democracy was dead. No one would be in any doubt about what had happened. What Varoufakis dreaded was that the government would back down without publicly acknowledging that the people's will had been subverted. Instead, the retreat would be dressed up as the only way to keep democracy alive. Acquiescing to the demands of the troika meant that the result of the referendum – which Tsipras had called and won precisely to resist those demands – was moot, but at least Greek democracy would live to fight another day. That is what happened. Tsipras stayed in office and won the next election. Varoufakis ended up writing his memoirs.

Varoufakis had been a child in Greece during the time of the colonels. He writes of their rule with utter contempt. Yet he respects them for one thing: they did not hide what they were about. When they came to power, their first move was to take control of the state television channels. He recalls: 'They had at least bothered to broadcast a picture of the Greek flag ... accompanied by military music.' [11] In the present state of Greece, television stations still play an important propaganda role, but what matters is what is kept *off* the screens. The government and the banks do what they can to prevent the spread of bad news. Because there are now so many other sources of information on the internet, the news spreads anyway. But a proliferation of news sources makes it harder to know what is really going on. People gravitate towards what they want to hear, so no one is any the wiser. That was not possible in 1967. Then there was no choice but to hear the worst.

The colonels marked their coup by making sure everyone understood what had changed. If Varoufakis is right, a twenty-first century coup is marked by the attempt to conceal what has changed. No one knows the truth. Democracy is dead! Long live democracy!

However, the story of Greek democracy did not start in the second half of the twentieth century. It goes much further back. Athens was the birthplace of democracy. For that reason it was also the birthplace of the anti-democratic coup. Modern representative democracy is far removed from the direct democracy that existed in ancient Athens more than two thousand years ago. Then it was a system founded on slavery, reserved for men only and built around face-to-face interactions. Politics was a rough business and it required ordinary citizens to be up for the fight. It suited a society in a near-permanent state of war. Democratic politics in the ancient world was tumultuous, time-consuming and often very violent.

Yet in one respect ancient Athens resembles contemporary Athens. After it had been around for a while, ancient Athenian democracy became set in its ways. It grew middle-aged. Towards the end of the fifth century BCE, having been in existence for nearly a century, democracy in Athens was working poorly. The state was blundering its way through a long war with Sparta and it was running out of money. The ordinary people, who bore the brunt of the incompetence of the leading citizens, were becoming increasingly angry and alarmed. Demagogues were stirring the pot. Yet democracy remained the only game in town. In the words of one historian of Athens in this period:

There is inefficiency and corruption in this democracy but the demos finds it worthwhile to put up with this in order to get its benefits. The demagogues are much less competent than clever young men would be in running the country but again they add to the demos' pleasure because they strengthen the democracy and increase the benefits. Therefore they are not to be got rid of. In fact it is no use hoping to change any details, however much in need of change they may be. All minor points are necessary side effects of democracy and since democracy cannot be shifted, with all its weaknesses, it must be accepted.[12]

Democracy looked immune to failure: nothing was bad enough that it couldn't be put down to the wear and tear of this way of doing politics. If there was no alternative to democracy, there was no alternative to putting up with it. *Plus ça change.*

Then, suddenly, a coup came. Following the fall-out of a military disaster in Sicily two years previously, a group of young Athenian aristocrats took over the state by force in the summer of 411 BCE. A new constitution was drawn up and prominent defenders of the old regime were sent into exile or assassinated. Authority was concentrated in a group known as the Four Hundred. The only way to join the group was to be rich enough to work for the government without pay, because salaries for public office were suspended. This group tried to pretend that democracy had not been abandoned altogether by endorsing a larger group of 5,000 soldier-citizens to ratify their decisions. It was lip service. No one was fooled. Democracy had given way to oligarchy. Power was in the hands of a privileged clique, backed up by violence.

Four hundred is far too few for a democracy. But it is enough for the people in charge to fall out among themselves. Divided between the conservatives, who wanted to kill democracy once and for all, and the moderates, who wished to keep it on life support, the oligarchs were fatally split. The moderates prevailed and they soon returned some real power to the 5,000. Then, following an unexpected naval triumph over the Spartans a year after the coup, full democracy was restored. The demagogues, who had always been the most strident defenders of democracy, managed to outbid the moderates. They persuaded the 5,000 that a final victory over the Spartans could still be theirs, if only they would put their faith back in the democracy that had been stolen from them, which meant putting their faith back in the demagogues.

The old constitution was reinstated, but a new law was added which read: 'I shall kill by word or by deed, by vote and with my own hand, if I can, anyone who subverts the democracy at Athens ... If anyone else kills such a person I will regard him as blameless before the gods and demons as having killed an enemy of the Athenian people.' In fact, the demagogues had misled the people: within a few years the long war with Sparta would be lost. But democracy in Athens survived for the best part of another century.

Ancient Athenian democracy was a robust and battle-hardened political system. It worked well enough to endure even when it was working badly. So when it failed, the failure had to be unambiguous: the coup of 411 was a hostile takeover by armed enemies of the regime. In that respect, it resembled the coup of 1967. The difference was that ancient Athenian democracy was strong enough to bounce back quickly. Within a year, the oligarchs were gone and the law had been changed to threaten anyone thinking of having another go with instant death.

In this way ancient Athenian democracy was able to survive its mid-life crisis, at a time when death in middle age was far more common than it is now. It showed its resilience again in 404 BCE, when defeat to Sparta resulted in power being put in the hands of a military junta of thirty. The arrangement lasted just eight months before democracy was restored, following a pitched battle for control of the city. Violence was defeated by more violence. The members of the junta were killed or sent into exile. Others who had tacitly co-operated with the regime were granted an amnesty, in perhaps the first 'peace and reconciliation' process in recorded history. The beneficiaries included the philosopher Socrates, who had been lukewarm in his condemnation of the junta. In due course it was decided that Socrates was still a dangerous influence and the restored democracy decided to kill him, too, following one of the most notorious show trials in history. Ancient Athenian democracy knew how to defend itself.

By contrast, Greek democracy in 1967 was weak, which is what allowed it to fail so quickly. It was built on sand. The coup succeeded in its own terms by bringing an end to the weakness its perpetrators claimed to abhor. But one sort of weakness was simply replaced with another. The colonels held on for nearly seven years. They eventually lost power when they fell out among themselves, paralysed by their inability to manage the consequences of the 1973 oil crisis and unable to stem the growing discontent of young Greeks, especially students. When the regime sent tanks into Athens Polytechnic in late 1973 to end a student sit-in, it was a sign not of strength but of inadequacy. The following year the colonels fatally mismanaged a military crisis in Cyprus, allowing Turkey to gain control of part of the island. Faced with the prospect of all-out war, democracy was soon restored. It had been strengthened by the long hiatus. People knew that the alternatives were worse.

Present-day Greek democracy has little of the wild drama of the ancient world and almost none of the violence. The country is not currently at war, so neither a military disaster, which almost destroyed ancient Athenian democracy, nor a military triumph, which restored it, is anywhere near at hand. Rich young men are more likely to emigrate, or to spend their time on Instagram, than to take up arms against the state. Even in the miserable condition in which Greece currently finds itself, most people have better things to do with their time than play for their lives in politics.

The closest contemporary Greek democracy has come to collapse was towards the end of 2011, when the elected government in Athens was unable to agree steps to address the growing debt crisis. A new prime minister, Lucas Papademos, was sworn in without ever having stood for election. He was a former banker and economic adviser to the outgoing prime minister, George Papandreou, son of the man whom the colonels had chased over the rooftops in 1967. Papademos sought to govern through a cabinet of economists and other experts, working to reform the Greek economy in line with the demands of the ECB in order to keep the country in the Eurozone. It was a takeover by technocrats. His government lasted just five months before it too failed to resolve the impasse. The army did not step in. Instead, it was decided to hold fresh elections, which gave Syriza its chance. In May 2017 Papademos was the victim of a failed assassination attempt, when a letter bomb exploded in his car. He suffered only minor injuries.

Greek democracy today is relatively battle-hardened, having been around for nearly half a century.

Democracy remains the default condition of Greek politics, so it continues to work even when it is working badly. It is the only game in town. Elections still take place and public opinion is unconstrained. Dissent is not just permitted, it is more or less ubiquitous. The hiatus of 2011–12 was even briefer than the ones at the end of the fifth century BCE. However, contemporary Greek democracy is nothing like the ancient version. It has no public contests of will to determine who is really in charge, with the losers facing death or exile. Most of the important action takes place behind the scenes. To discover what's really going on, we have to wait for the key players to write their memoirs. Even then we can't be sure they are telling the truth. There are no impartial witnesses.

Few in Greece today seriously believe that they are living under a dictatorship. If that were to happen, everyone would know the difference. But is Greece still a functioning democracy? It has the appearance of a democracy, but appearances can be deceptive. The present Greek government has to bend to the will of the troika, the economy remains on life support, and the people bear the consequences. Conspiracy theories are rife but no conspiracy ever fully comes out into the open, unlike in 1967, or in 411 BCE, when the conspirators had to go public with what they were up to. There is cheap talk of coups – a coup by the bankers, a coup by the technocrats, a coup by the Germans – but these are metaphorical coups. They are not for real. No one's hands tremble in quite the way that Papandreou's did in 1967.

* * *

WHAT MAKES A COUP real? In 1968 Edward Luttwak, a young American political scientist, published a slim volume called *Coup D'État: A Practical Handbook*. It was, in its author's words, a kind of cookery book for political subversion, laying out what steps were needed to take over the state by force. Luttwak claimed to be a dispassionate guide to the practicalities. 'Just as in cooking a bouillabaisse,' he wrote, 'one needs the right sort of fish to start with' – though he warned that the dangers of getting it wrong would be more serious than having 'to eat out of a tin'.[13] Luttwak wanted to lay down some rules to avoid the dish getting burnt. None the less, one ostensible reason for showing how to do it was to indicate how to stop it: if democrats knew what were the right ingredients they could try to make sure they did not fall into the wrong hands.

Luttwak argued that it was important to understand the difference between a coup and a palace revolution. The latter was a private affair played out within a tiny elite, as when Roman emperors were murdered by their mothers or their bodyguards. All that happens then is one unaccountable ruler ends up being replaced by another. The key to survival under those circumstances is simply to get out of the way. A coup, by contrast, is based on the idea that to govern is to secure control of the machinery of the state, including all the people who work for it. Neutral civil servants and other public officials are not free to turn their backs or avert their eyes. They have to sign up to the new regime. That's why a coup takes careful planning and forceful execution. In Luttwak's words: 'A coup consists of the infiltration of a small but critical segment of the state apparatus, which is then used to displace the government from its control of the remainder.'[14]

This process turns the people into bystanders: all

they can do is look on from a distance. In a well-planned coup, things will need to happen quickly enough to ensure that the wider population does not have time to mobilise in response. That is why it is so important to take over the key communication points and to start broadcasting propaganda for the new regime. Also, do it at night, when most people are asleep. A coup d'état needs to become a fait accompli as fast as possible. Luttwak thought that a coup had little chance of success in a country where the population was strongly attached to democracy and easily roused to defend it. Under those conditions, broadcasting martial music wouldn't be enough. If democracy is weak, there is little worth defending. But if it commands popular support, then it will be hard to prise the state away from the government, because the people will not stand for it. They will fight back.

Luttwak contended that the age of the coup was effectively over in most advanced Western democracies. One had been tried in France in 1961, when General de Gaulle faced an attempt by disgruntled French army officers in Algeria to overthrow the republic by force. The plotters believed that de Gaulle was planning to sell them out by granting Algeria independence. They mounted their rebellion on the night of 21 April, by chance the exact same date as the successful Greek coup six years later. But in this case, it didn't work. The plotters got comprehensively quashed.

Why did they fail? First, Algeria was too far from Paris and the conspirators were not able to gain control of the key communication points or government offices. Second, de Gaulle was able to rally the French people to defend the state against an armed takeover. Rumours quickly circulated that the Algerian army was planning to land parachutists on airfields outside Paris with instructions to advance on the city. De Gaulle went on television to declare: 'In the name of France, I order that all means – I repeat all means – be employed to bar the way everywhere to these men until they are brought down. I forbid every Frenchman, and in the first place every soldier, to carry out any of their orders.' This message was re-broadcast via radio to French settlers in Algeria. In his memoirs, de Gaulle later wrote: 'Everyone, everywhere, heard my words. In metropolitan France, there was not one who did not watch or listen. In Algeria, a million transistors were tuned in. From then on, the revolt met with a passive resistance on the spot which became hourly more explicit.'[15]

The French Fifth Republic, with de Gaulle at its head, was not much of a democracy: the president exercised pseudo-monarchical powers and wielded enormous personal authority. 'Basically, the Republic is me,' is how de Gaulle liked to put it, echoing Louis XIV. But it was enough of a democracy – the French people had endorsed it overwhelmingly in a referendum three years earlier and they were willing to defend it. Where democracy has popular legitimacy, the people will not remain as bystanders when it is under direct attack. For that reason, coups are often seen as symptoms of democratic backwardness. They are only possible in nations where democracy has not had time to develop roots.

Part of de Gaulle's success in facing down the Algerian rebellion was to make it sound fundamentally un-French, more suited to the goings-on in a banana republic than a modern democracy. In his television address he called it not a '*coup*' but a '*pronunciamiento*', deliberately reducing it, in the words of one biographer, 'to the level of a Latin American comic opera'.[16] As democracy gets stronger, the possibility of a coup should start to sound more and more like a joke.

A coup d'état is not the only sort of coup, however. Luttwak's cookery book lists the different ingredients for the end of democracy, but he was only interested in making one kind of dish: an armed takeover of the state. What about the other ways in which a democracy can be subverted? The American political scientist Nancy Bermeo has recently identified six different varieties of coup, of which the coup d'état is only one. The others are:

- 'Executive coups', when those already in power suspend democratic institutions.
- 'Election-day vote fraud', when the electoral process is fixed to produce a particular result.
- 'Promissory coups', when democracy is taken over by people who then hold elections to legitimise their rule.
- 'Executive aggrandisement', when those already in power chip away at democratic institutions without ever overturning them.
- 'Strategic election manipulation', when elections fall short of being free and fair but also fall short of being stolen outright.[17]

In none of these kinds of coup is it necessary for soldiers to sneak in at night to arrest the government. That's because the coup is either being undertaken by the government itself or it is being dressed up as something other than a coup. Most often it is both.

Whichever way you slice and dice the different types of coup, there is one fundamental distinction between them: some coups need to make clear that democracy is over in order to succeed; and some coups need to pretend that democracy is still intact. Coups d'état fall into the first category. But the others tend to fall into the second, especially the latter three. These coups are about keeping up appearances. People manipulate elections because the appearance of victory at the ballot box is what gives them the authority to rule. Promissory coups and executive aggrandisement require that the appearance of democracy be maintained, because the success of the coup depends on people believing that democracy continues to exist. For some kinds of coup, democracy is not the enemy. It provides the cover for subversion, which makes it the plotters' friend.

By fixing on coups d'état, we get a misleading impression of where and when coups are likely to happen. Bermeo notes that armed coups, executive coups and stolen elections have long been in decline as methods of political change around the world – as democracy becomes more established, it gets harder and harder to overturn it by force or outright fraud. During the 1960s Greek democracy was so weak that it had versions of all three: the election of 'violence and fraud' in 1961, when the vote was widely believed to have been stolen; the 'royalist coup' in 1965, when the king replaced the elected government without a democratic mandate; and finally, the colonels' coup d'état in 1967. Contemporary Greece does not look remotely vulnerable to a similar sequence of events. In established democracies, there is very little scope for cowing the people into submission when an explicit power grab is underway.

But the scope for the other sorts of coup is greater once democracy has become the default. The more democracy is taken for granted, the more chance there is to subvert it without having to overthrow it. In particular, executive aggrandisement – when elected strongmen chip away at democracy while paying lip service to it – looks like being the biggest threat to democracy in the twenty-first century. It appears to be happening in, among other places, India, Turkey, the Philippines, Ecuador, Hungary and Poland; and it is possible that it is happening in the United States as well. The problem is that it can be difficult to know for sure. The big difference between a coup d'état and these other sorts of coups is that the former is an all-or-nothing event and the latter are incremental processes. One sort of coup will succeed or fail in a matter of hours. The others take place over a period of years without anyone being sure whether they have succeeded or not. It becomes much harder to draw the line. More than that: while people are waiting for the real coup to reveal itself, the bit-by-bit coup may have been long underway.

Bermeo notes that a big problem with incremental coups is knowing how to oppose them. Democracies that 'erode rather than shatter often lack the spark that ignites an effective call to action'.[18] There is no single moment to rally the forces of democracy against the threat that confronts it. Instead, political infighting produces a series of disjointed confrontations that each side sees differently: while the opponents of the regime shout, 'Coup!', its defenders say that those accusations are hyperbole and hysteria. Lawyers and journalists who see themselves as the last line of defence against the subversion of democracy can be recast by the other side as just another group of 'special interests', claiming the benefits of democracy for themselves.

One part of Luttwak's definition of a coup still holds. If democracy is going to be subverted, then it is essential that the people as a whole remain bystanders. No coup can succeed if the public rises up against it. At that point, the only alternatives are the collapse of the coup or a civil war for real. However, there is more than one way to keep the public quiet. A coup d'état works on the basis of intimidation and coercion. But a coup that hides behind the workings of democracy can hope to get by on the public's innate passivity. In most functioning democracies, the people are bystanders much of the time anyway. They watch on as political decisions are taken on their behalf by elected representatives who then ask for their assent at election time. If that's what democracy has become, it provides excellent cover for the attempt to undermine democracy, because the two look remarkably similar.

Contemporary political science has devised a range of terms to describe this state of affairs: 'audience democracy', 'spectator democracy', 'plebiscitary democracy'. These terms might be too mild: 'zombie democracy' might be better. The basic idea is that the people are simply watching a performance in which their role is to give or withhold their applause at the appropriate moments. Democratic politics has become an elaborate show, needing ever more characterful performers to hold the public's attention. The increasing reliance on referendums in many democracies fits this pattern. A referendum looks democratic but it is not. The spectators get dragged on stage to say a simple yes or no to a proposition they have played no part in devising. Then the politicians get back to the business of deciding what they meant by what they said, while the voters look on, many of them growing frustrated at not having a chance to play a further part. If necessary, another referendum can be called to get them to agree to whatever it was they were taken to have decided first time round. Not every referendum is evidence of a promissory coup. But referendums are one way to manage it.

What makes referendums particularly effective in this context is that they can be presented as the antithesis of the subversion of democracy. What could be more democratic than asking the people as a whole what they think? A direct question gets a direct answer. Often, the answer comes back as a demand for more democracy. The Brexit vote in the United Kingdom was advertised as an example of direct democracy in action. It was won with the aid of a slogan that reinforced the appeal of direct democracy: 'Take back control'. Yet the result was to hand more control to the British executive, whose job it became to deliver on what the British people wanted. The executive is now locked in a tussle with the British parliament to try to ensure that it retains those powers even after Brexit has happened. No one could argue that the Brexit referendum was a successful instance of an executive coup, given that the prime minister who called it lost his job as a result. What it does show is how easily the popular demand for more democracy can end up having the opposite effect.

The old-fashioned coup d'état is far from dead everywhere, however. In late 2017, President Robert Mugabe of Zimbabwe was removed from office by a coup that followed much of the classic pattern, albeit in slow motion. Generals in full uniform seized the TV stations and announced their intention to prosecute 'criminals'. Tanks appeared on the streets of the capital, Harare. Only Mugabe's faltering speech in which he initially refused to resign, delivered as he sat flanked by baffled-looking military men riffling through their papers for the correct text, deviated from the script. But Mugabe quit three days later anyway.

Egypt's recent flirtation with democracy after the Arab Spring ended with an event that had all the hallmarks of a military coup. In 2013, the head of the armed forces overthrew the elected government of Mohammed Morsi, arrested its leading members and suspended the constitution. Presidential elections were held the following year. General Abdul Fatah el-Sisi, the man who had orchestrated the coup, won with 97 per cent of the vote.

No matter how bad things get, it seems very unlikely that America will go down the same route. The United States is too rich, too old, too set in its ways for this kind of politics. Contemporary America is a very different society from contemporary Egypt, never mind present-day Zimbabwe. Trump's admiration for various strongmen around the world, including Sisi, does not make him their equivalent. But America is also a very different society now compared to how it was in the past. America was Egypt once.

Present-day Egypt is a relatively youthful society: its median age is around 24, which is roughly that of the US in 1930. Egypt is not a wealthy society: its per capita GDP is about $4000, which is roughly the same as it was in the US in 1930. Unemployment in Egypt is currently high at around 15 per cent, similar to where it was in the US in 1930 (though in the American case, thanks to the Great Depression, it was about to go much higher). Of course, there are big differences. Many of America's democratic institutions were already much more robust and battle-hardened by the 1930s than Egypt's are today. The army is a far more significant force in contemporary Egypt than it was in 1930s America, where there was no army to speak of. There was no American equivalent to the Muslim Brotherhood either. None the less, if we are to argue that a coup in Egypt has lessons for Western democracy, we need to apply that lesson correctly. There could have been a coup in the US during the 1930s – there were demagogues and putative dictators like Huey Long who appeared willing to take their chances, had the chance arisen. Democracy might have collapsed. The social conditions made it possible, even if the institutional constraints made it unlikely. Nineteen thirties America has more in common with twenty-first century Egypt than twenty-first century America has in common with either.

Democracy did ultimately collapse across western Europe during the interwar period. By the end of the 1930s there were very few democracies left outside of the English-speaking world. Men in uniforms had replaced men in suits almost everywhere else. When we talk today about the danger of going back to the 1930s, this is what we have in mind: a domino effect of democratic failure around the world. So it is important to be clear: a repeat of the 1930s is much more likely in some places than in others. The places where it is least likely are the places where it happened first time around. Germany today has almost nothing in common politically with Germany in 1933. France is a different country than it was even fifty years ago. Italy is not going to succumb to military rule any time soon. Even Greece looks to have left that kind of politics behind.

The places where it is hardest to be sure are the ones that stand somewhere between today's US and Egypt. For instance, present-day Turkey is a democracy with relatively deep roots. It has been ruled by elected governments for most of its history since the founding of the modern republic in 1923. At the same time, that history has been repeatedly punctuated by military coups. There was one in 1960, another in 1971, and another in 1980. In each case the army moved in to replace the elected government.

The 1980 coup followed the classic model described by Luttwak, with a junta of six generals taking power overnight, sending tanks on to the streets of the capital and arresting leading members of the government. None the less, these were also promissory coups, given that the army promised to restore democracy as soon as order had been achieved. The Turkish armed forces have traditionally seen themselves as guardians of the secular constitution, against those who would try to subvert it in the name of Islam. Each coup put civilians back in charge after a couple of years, though this was always on sufferance: the generals stood ready to step back in if things did not go their way.

There have been no further military coups since 1980, though in 1997 the army demanded the resignation of the prime minister and got it, without having to use force. The hint was enough, leading some to dub this the first 'postmodern coup'. In 2002, Recep Erdogan's Justice and Development Party (AKP) won decisively in elections that were seen as a rebuke against military interference. Five years later Erdogan emerged victorious from a showdown with the army over his nomination of an Islamist confidant as president. The generals warned that they were once again ready to intervene to protect the republic from an Islamist takeover, but Erdogan denounced the threat of military interference and won overwhelming popular support. In the years that followed, Erdogan undertook a series of reforms that strengthened his position and further eroded the strict division between state and religion. He made these moves in the name of democracy.

Then, on the night of 15 July 2016, Turkey woke up to find itself in the middle of another military coup. Tanks rumbled through the streets of Istanbul, soldiers were sent in to take control of key transport and communication points and there were moves to arrest leading members of the government, including Erdogan. This time, the plot failed. Erdogan took a leaf out of de Gaulle's playbook, updated for the age of social media, and appeared online in the early hours of the morning to denounce the coup and demand that ordinary Turks take to the streets to prevent it. His call was heeded and within twelve hours the coup had collapsed in the face of massive popular resistance. Though Erdogan had been increasingly unpopular in the months before the coup, many of his political opponents took his side in the face of a threatened return to military rule.

In the days that followed, Erdogan used this support to cement his grip on power. The coup was blamed on his former ally and now arch-rival, Fethullah Gulen, whose supporters were accused of having subverted significant parts of the military and the education system in order to foment the overthrow of the state. Erdogan purged the army and the universities. He jailed large numbers of opposition politicians, journalists and educators. In 2017 he initiated and narrowly won a referendum on greatly enhanced powers for the presidency, the office he now held. The measures proposed included the abolition of military courts, a popular reform. He undertook all these moves in the name of democracy.

The current state of Turkish politics shows how blurred the lines can become between democracy and its subversion, once democracy is established as the default condition of politics. It is clear that the coup failed for the reasons Luttwak foresaw: where the public refuse to remain bystanders, the military will find it very hard to overthrow a democracy. The people saved the regime. However, the popular defence of democracy has also created the conditions for massive executive aggrandisement. Erdogan has greatly enhanced his own personal power as a result. He has been careful to frame this as a way of protecting democracy against the possibility of future military takeover.

At the same time, Erdogan's actions have become the subject of wide-ranging conspiracy theories, based on the assumption that in politics the only question worth asking is: who benefits? For many observers, the events of the night of 15 July were simply too convenient to be plausible. Could Gulen, an exiled cleric living in rural Pennsylvania, really have masterminded such an elaborate plot? The person who benefitted was Erdogan. On this logic, it follows that he must have been the person behind the coup. The failed coup d'état turns into a cover story for the real subversion of democracy.

The attempted coup of July 2016 can simultaneously be held up as evidence of two diametrically opposed threats to democracy. If it is taken at face value, the threat comes from the military: Turkish democracy is still weak enough that it could be overthrown by force. But if the coup is assumed to be fake, then the threat comes from the democratically elected government: Turkish democracy is now secure enough that popular support becomes the cover for would-be autocrats to hide behind. There is nothing – no event, no argument, no piece of evidence – that can determine to the satisfaction of all parties which view is correct.

It is possible that Turkey is now a society in which a military coup is no longer a realistic prospect. That is not something that can be proven because it is not possible to prove a negative. It can only be disproven by a successful coup. This is a looking-glass world in which nothing is necessarily what it seems. A failed military takeover does not mean that the threat of a coup d'état is real. It could mean that democracy faces no such threat, in which case the real risk to democracy is of being subverted from within.

There is no cookbook to help make sense of what has happened, because the same ingredients cooked in the same way can produce two totally different dishes.

The US is not Turkey any more than it is Egypt. None

the less there are lessons here for even the most secure democracies. Seen through the looking glass, things that were once threats to democracy can become bulwarks in its defence, while its one-time supports can become the biggest threats. Propping up democracy may be a recipe for its ultimate failure.

Take military–civilian relations. In a well-established democracy, it is understood that the generals must do what their civilian leaders tell them. The alternative is generals refusing to take orders, which is tantamount to a coup. But in a state in which the routine acceptance of democratic rule is being used to conceal growing concentrations of power at the centre, the reverse may be true. The capacity of the executive to command the obedience of the soldiers may be one of the things that facilitates the incremental demise of democracy.

The legal scholar Bruce Ackerman has characterised the last fifty years of American presidential politics as a series of power-grabs by the executive. The biggest involves the politicisation of the military, which has been increasingly co-opted into executive rule. Faced with a recalcitrant Congress, presidents turn to soldiers to get things done. Ackerman sees two dangers. One is that a subservient high command might greatly expand the powers of an extremist presidency by doing what it is told. The other is that the president ends up doing what he is told by his generals, who have become an indispensable part of the administration. The commander-in-chief then becomes a figurehead for what is essentially military rule. Are the generals obeying politicians or the politicians obeying generals? Once the lines gets blurred, it is hard to know for sure.

Ackerman traces this process through a series of presidencies. It has been driven by regular emergencies running alongside growing frustration with partisan politics. Bill Clinton looked to enhance the discretionary power of the presidency to allow him to undertake executive initiatives in the face of a Republican-controlled Congress; George W. Bush did it in the aftermath of 9/11 to facilitate the War on Terror; Obama did it to prosecute his own war on Al Qaeda and ISIS. Ackerman characterises this as part of the increasing lawlessness of democratic politics in the US, as presidents follow the path of least resistance. It is not the same as a coup. None of these presidents had any intention of subverting the constitution. But what happens if you end up with a president who has no great attachment to the constitution and sees any resistance to executive rule as tantamount to a betrayal of democracy? What happens when that president staffs his administration with retired generals? What happens when you get President Trump?

Writing in 2010, Ackerman speculated about the danger of some future 'President Rightist insisting that the nation can no longer tolerate tens of millions of immigrants in our midst, and he has no choice but to detain and deport them with "all deliberate speed"'. He also conjured up a possible 'President Leftist, demonizing the banks, condemning them for a great conspiracy ... and demanding their immediate nationalization in the name of the people'.[19] Under these conditions, the situation becomes much more fraught. Not only soldiers but civil servants and other public officials have to decide where they stand. In a modern state, unlike in ancient Rome, it is not possible to look the other way and hope the storm will pass. Either you do what you are told or you don't. The problem is that once democratic politics has been subject to executive aggrandisement, to refuse to assent is to risk being tarred as an enemy of democracy.

There are still options. Public servants can resign, though then the risk is that they will simply be replaced by more pliable officials, or not replaced at all. The more extreme step is to stay in post but refuse to obey. The generals could not have declined to hand over the nuclear codes to Trump before his inauguration without undermining the very basis of democracy. But they could potentially refuse to follow his orders to activate them. What if Trump makes a reckless executive decision about the use of nuclear force that threatens the survival of the American republic, and indeed the world? Is it possible to disobey in the name of democracy?

Modern American history does provide at least one precedent. In the dying days of the Nixon presidency in the summer of 1974 the Secretary of Defense James Schlesinger became so alarmed by the president's state of mind – Nixon was seriously depressed and drinking heavily – that he instructed the military not to act on presidential orders, especially with regard to nuclear weapons, unless first cleared by either himself or Secretary of State Henry Kissinger. He also drew up plans to deploy troops in Washington in the event that it was not possible to arrange a peaceful presidential transition. This kind of behaviour exists in that murky space where a coup is not really a coup. Under President Trump, that space has grown.

What makes it even murkier is that Schlesinger only revealed his decision years after the event, when the heat had gone out of the situation. At the time he had to do it all in secret, because any attempt to play his hand in public would have exposed him to the charge of plotting a coup. If the subversion of democracy is taking place under the cover of democracy, then the subversion of the subversion has to take place under cover, too. Nothing is revealed. This is the mirror image of the world of the coup d'état described by Luttwak. Whereas a successful coup once required that everyone should know what's going on, now both a coup and a counter-coup require that as few people understand what is happening as possible.

This netherworld of conspiracy and subterfuge can be easier to describe in political fiction than in political science. It depends on things that are only known to the participants, who may or may not let slip what really happened long after the event has passed. The easiest way to picture it is to try to imagine what the participants might have been up to. We sometimes have to make it up.

The *Guardian* journalist Jonathan Freedland, writing under the pseudonym Sam Bourne, maps out one way it could go in his 2017 novel *To Kill the President*.[20] The book is totally absurd and horribly compelling. In this scenario a President Rightist, loosely based on President Trump, threatens to unleash a nuclear strike on North Korea in a moment of pique. His Secretary of Defense and Chief of Staff decide they have no alternative but to try to kill him, because all other options – resigning, refusing to obey or public denunciation – would simply make the problem worse, by giving the president an excuse to round on his enemies. In the meantime, the president's chief strategist, loosely based on Steve Bannon, gets wind of the assassination attempt and decides to use it to frame an Islamist conspiracy, allowing for a further crackdown on anyone perceived as un-American. All of this happens behind closed doors, under the cover of the deafening chatter of the social media age. While members of the public are screaming conspiracy and coup from all sides, the real acts of subversion happen in the places social media cannot reach. When accusations of conspiracy are everywhere, the space to hide a true conspiracy expands, because no one can see the forest for the trees.

It doesn't just have to be a President Rightist, and it doesn't only happen in the age of Twitter. In Chris Mullin's novel *A Very British Coup*, written in 1982 and set in 1989, a Prime Minister Leftist wins a UK general election on a manifesto committed to full-scale nationalisation, nuclear disarmament and quitting NATO.[21] The forces of the establishment conspire to stop him, by spreading poison in the popular press, destabilising the economy and encouraging covert acts of disobedience in the military. None of this is revealed for what it is – the plotters are careful to conceal their actions behind the rough and tumble of democratic politics. The coup succeeds because no one knows that it has happened – the prime minister resigns on the grounds of ill health, and is replaced by his deputy, who happens to be in the pay of the secret services. Of course, the public has its suspicions, but the public always has its suspicions. The drama of democratic life absorbs the evidence without anyone being any the wiser.

Freedland's novel is closer to home for now because the election of a President Rightist came to pass. Mullin was a would-be Labour MP on the left of the party in the 1980s and an ally of the young Jeremy Corbyn. It is unlikely that Mullin ever imagined Corbyn would be the person who might put his fiction to the test. Both men were acolytes of Tony Benn, who was for many years the British left's best hope. Benn never came that close to becoming prime minister. As I write, the prospect of a Corbyn prime ministership is very real. Something like it will happen somewhere eventually. Bernie Sanders came close in the 2016 US presidential election. Jean-Luc Mélenchon came close in the French presidential election of 2017. At some point a President or Prime Minister Leftist will win an election in a leading democracy and challenge the political establishment to do its worst.

When that occurs, will we get a very American, a very French or a very British coup? The answer is that, whatever happens, there will be no agreement about what has really happened. Did we get a very Greek coup in 2015? Where coups once brought clarity – if nothing else – talk of coups is now the enemy of clarity. One side sees a coup. The other side sees democracy working as it should. This is not simply a question of left v. right. Trump came into office on a promise to abandon NATO if it didn't start relieving America's burdens. The soldiers who help run his administration persuaded him otherwise. Does that mean democracy has been subverted because the president's will has been obstructed by unelected powers? Or is it a sign of democracy working as it should because the president's will has been moderated by the forces of restraint? There can be no answer to that question that satisfies all sides. Meanwhile, the dialogue of the deaf continues.

Weak democracies are vulnerable to coup d'états because their institutions cannot absorb a frontal assault. Strong democracies are relatively immune to a frontal assault because their institutions are resilient. As a result, the assault on stable democracies comes from the sides. Some of it gets deflected into idle chatter – the constant talk of betrayal, failure and crisis that is the background noise of partisan politics. Some of it gets pushed under the surface and behind the scenes, where only the adults in the room can be sure what really took place, and even they don't agree. These phenomena feed off each other. Idle talk about the end of democracy is excellent cover for incremental assaults on democracy to hide behind. Meanwhile, the incremental assaults help to feed the talk of failure, without anyone being sure.

Strong democracies have all the advantages over weak democracies except one: weak democracies know when they have failed. Failure looks like Greece in 1967. It doesn't look like that any more. Now, if we have coups, they arrive without the coup de grace. There is no before and after. There is only the murky space between.

A SUCCESSFUL COUP D'ÉTAT requires a successful conspiracy. It must be secret, tightknit and a surprise to those on the receiving end. Only when the coup is underway do the conspirators show their hand. The demise of the coup d'état spells the end of that kind of conspiracy – in a well-established democracy the likelihood of success is too remote. But the decline of the coup d'état means the inevitable rise of conspiracy theories, which conjure up the conspiracies that never truly reveal their hand.

The existence of what we now call conspiracy theories is nothing new. They have been around forever. Ancient Athenian democracy was rife with suspicions of plots and secret clubs bent on its destruction. It is the lifeblood of democracy to imagine that hidden cliques are trying to subvert it. There are two reasons for this. First, democracy allows ordinary people to speak their minds, and what is often on people's minds is the feeling that they are being screwed over. If it's not obvious who's doing the screwing over, then it must be because the culprits are covering their tracks. Second, the culprits do try to cover their tracks. What keeps conspiracy theories going is the intermittent emergence into the light of genuine conspiracies. In 412 BCE those claiming that Athenian democracy was about to be taken over by a clique of oligarchs working for the Spartans were peddling wild rumours. A year later they were telling it like it was.

Modern democracy is no different. Though the

term conspiracy theory is a relatively recent invention – it only gained wide currency after the 1960s, driven in part by the wave of suspicion that built up after the Kennedy assassination – the phenomenon it describes long predates its coinage. The evolution of democratic politics through the nineteenth and twentieth centuries was accompanied by the persistent suspicion that it was all a sham: secret elites continued to pull the strings behind the scenes. This suspicion was fuelled by the fact that representative democracy does empower elites and they do conduct much of their business behind closed doors. Any political system that trumpets the value of openness while holding on to its secrets will create the space in which conspiracy theories can flourish.

Under a tyranny, the conspiracy theorists are usually the people inside the regime, who see plots against them everywhere. For the victims of oppressive regimes, conspiracy theories have little value because the truth doesn't have anywhere to hide – deceit and violence are how the state does its business. What you see is what you get, even if what you get is a lie. In democracies, it is the gap between the promise of popular government and the persistence of personal connections at the top that gives the conspiracy theorists their ammunition.

Of course, not every citizen of a democracy is a conspiracy theorist, for the simple reason that representative democracy is not just a sham. Elites can be constrained by institutions designed to limit their reach. The wealthy and the well born don't always get away with it. Many people do feel the benefits of democracy, both because of the dignity it confers and the material advantages it can bring. Conspiracy theorists tend to be the ones who feel that, despite this, the benefits are not reaching them. In any democracy there will be winners and losers. In the words of two American political scientists, Joe Parent and Joe Uscinski, 'conspiracy theories are for losers'.[22]

This is borne out by the historical data. Parent and Uscinski's study of the prevalence of political conspiracy theories in the United States over the past century shows that they tend to track the possession of power.[23] The people who feel excluded from power are far more likely to back the idea that it has been stolen from them by anti-democratic forces operating by subterfuge. The overall proportion of those who believe that democracy is in the grip of secret organisations is relatively stable: at any given moment it is likely that somewhere between a quarter and a third of Americans are willing to sign up to conspiracy theories of this kind. But who is willing to sign up, shifts according to which party occupies the White House.

When a Democrat is president, Republican voters are liable to think that the government is in the control of foreign agents, because the president is a secret communist, or a secret Muslim, or in some other way not a real American. When a Republican is president, then Democrats are liable to believe that democracy has been captured by Wall Street, or that the administration is in the pay of the oil industry. So when George W. Bush was president, Democrats were the conspiracy theorists; when Obama succeeded him, the roles were reversed and Republicans became the conspiracy theorists. If your side wins, democracy seems to make a lot more sense than if your side loses. Some people are bad losers. They take defeat as evidence that the system is being rigged against them. It requires a victory to change their minds.

The most persistent conspiracy theorists are the people who feel they can never win under the rules of democratic politics. A recent survey of UK voters showed that conspiracy theories are most prevalent among those who feel permanently disenfranchised.[24] If you support a party that has no chance of winning power – especially under a two-party, first-past-the-post system – democracy does appear biased against you. It will be worse if you support no party at all. An old anarchist slogan says that it doesn't matter who you vote for, the government always gets in. It is not just anarchists who think like that. Anyone who has lost faith in the possibility of political change is likely to believe voting is not worth the bother; anyone who stops voting is likely to find that the system ignores them because their views don't count.

This is potentially a vicious circle. None the less, it has limits. So long as enough voters are willing to see a victory for one side or the other as a win for them personally, democracy can keep functioning. The danger comes when the permanent losers outnumber the occasional winners – when conspiracy theory moves from being a minority pastime to a majority pursuit. We may be in the middle of just such a shift.

As a result, the twenty-first century could begin to look like the golden age of conspiracy theories. They seem to be everywhere at present. Some of this is an illusion, generated by the greater visibility that any crackpot idea can achieve in the era of the internet. Where once someone who thought the British royal family are lizards in human form would have had little chance of meeting anyone else who shared that view, now like-minded conspiracy theorists are just a click away from each other. This visibility does not mean that there are more of these ideas about than ever before, only that they are more likely to achieve a critical mass. The phenomenon of network effects, where something gains in value the more people use it, holds for bad ideas as well as good ones. The more people who subscribe to a conspiracy theory, the more point there is in joining them. Social networks provide safety in numbers.

But something else has changed. Conspiracy theories are no longer just for losers. The winners believe in them, too. Donald Trump embarked on his bid for national office by embracing one of the most persistent conspiracy theories about President Obama, that he was not an American citizen. The 'birther' movement was quintessential losers' politics: voters who believed that Obama did not speak for them latched on to the idea that he could not speak for them because he was a secret alien. Trump rode this idea most of the way to the White House, only half-heartedly ditching it as Election Day approached. But he did not ditch the mindset it represents, even after he won. Trump as president has continued to peddle conspiracy theories from the Oval Office. He accused his defeated opponent of having stolen the popular vote by widespread electoral fraud. He accused his critics in the mainstream media of deliberately creating fake news stories to discredit his presidency. He accused his predecessor of having tapped his phones. There was little or no evidence for any of this. Trump the winner was behaving as though he had lost. He did this in order to cement the terms on which he had won and keep himself firmly aligned with his core constituency.

After Trump's victory, defeated Democrats quickly turned from dismissing conspiracy theories about the old president to spreading them about the new one. He was soon engulfed by accusations that he was a stooge of the Russians. Trump and his acolytes fought back in the only way they knew how. They turned the conspiracy theories back on the Democrats. *They* were the ones in the power of the Russians. *They* were the ones faking the news. One reason it can seem conspiracy theories are everywhere at present is that the various sides are no longer taking it in turns to question the bona fides of the others. Now they are doing it simultaneously.

This is entirely characteristic of a period when populism has come to dominate democratic politics. The basic idea behind populism, whether from the left or the right, is that democracy has been stolen from the people by the elites. In order to claim it back, the elites have to be flushed out from their hiding places, where they conceal what they are up to by paying lip service to democracy. Conspiracy theory is the logic of populism. Trump's inaugural address was a concise expression of this line of thought. Its rhetoric aligned Trump with other populist leaders around the world, who frame politics in much the same way.

In Turkey, Erdogan's default explanation for political opposition to his rule is that his enemies are conspiring against the Turkish people. The conspirators include not just Gulen and his cronies, but the EU, the IMF and the 'interest rate lobby', which is shorthand for the Jews. In Poland, the Law and Justice Party (PiS) government repeatedly blames 'the system' for any problems it faces. This system is made up of unelected officials and institutions that have been infiltrated by the agents of foreign regimes. In the words of Jaroslaw Kazcynski, the co-founder and leader of PiS: 'This is about whether democracy is able to make decisions instead of a handful of people bought by foreigners and internal forces that don't serve Poland's interests.'[25] In India, Narendra Modi uses Twitter as much as Trump does to lambast those who are plotting his downfall, from foreign powers to the Indian 'deep state'. Meanwhile, Modi's opponents circulate ever-wilder conspiracy theories about him: his election victories were achieved by ballot-rigging; he is a Pakistani secret agent; he is a Jew. Populism promotes paranoia on all sides.

Once conspiracy theorising gets made into a governing philosophy, it becomes self-reinforcing. The voters no longer take it in turns to voice their suspicions that the system is rigged. Win or lose, all parties come to see democracy as concealing plots against them. How to break this cycle? It is very hard. One way might be for the real conspiracies to be pushed out into the open, finally proving someone right. But, as we have seen, coups are not what they used to be. Another would be for the fake conspiracy theories to be exposed as bogus, finally proving someone wrong. But that also rarely happens. The failed coup d'état in Turkey settled nothing because it confirmed everything that people on all sides wanted to believe. It was held up as evidence both that Erdogan was the victim of a conspiracy and that he was the agent of the same conspiracy.

In 2010 Lech Kazcynski, the Polish president and brother of Jaroslaw, died in a plane crash on his way to the Katyn forest, near Smolensk in western Russia, where he was due to commemorate the deaths of 20,000 Polish officers, murdered by agents of the Stalin regime in 1940. Jaroslaw and his supporters have placed the blame for the crash on 'the system', which in this case includes the Russians, the EU, the liberal establishment, the secret communists and the Jews. Numerous investigations have found no evidence that it was caused by anything other than pilot error in bad weather. It makes no difference. And were a further investigation now to find that there was evidence of Russian complicity in the disaster, it would make no difference, either. For anyone inclined to disagree, it would simply be proof that the new investigation was part of a government conspiracy. Increasingly, people will believe what they want to believe. Populist politics feeds off that phenomenon. It also fuels it.

If we want to find historical parallels for these features of contemporary politics, we can. But we need to look in the right place. It means stepping outside the twentieth century. The 1890s can offer a better guide to our current turmoil than the 1930s. The 1930s were the great age of conspiracies: a decade that began with the death throes of the Weimar Republic and ended with the Nazi–Soviet pact, had enough real plots to satisfy even the most suspicious minds. But the 1890s was the great age of conspiracy theories.

Populism itself is nothing new. It rises in democratic societies under particular conditions: economic distress, technological change, growing inequality and the absence of war. This is not the first time those conditions have held. It was true at the end of the nineteenth century, too, when democratic politics was roiled by another great wave of populist anger. Then as now, the anger was a fertile breeding ground for conspiracy theories on both sides of the political divide.

The 1890s are one of the very few periods in modern American history when the overall volume of conspiracy theories in circulation showed a notable increase. The other time, before now, came in the late 1940s and early 1950s, at the dawn of the Cold War, when the virus of McCarthyism spread through American public life and infected it with a paranoia that cut across the partisan divide. It is late nineteenth-century populism that provides a case study for what the historian Richard Hofstadter famously called 'the paranoid style in American politics'.[26] It's that same paranoid style that is at work today.

The parallels between then and now are many. The great populist backlash of the late nineteenth century was triggered by drawn-out economic distress. The American economy endured a lengthy period of economic stagnation from the 1870s onwards, which saw wages fall along with prices. Agricultural workers bore the brunt of the misery and they took out their resentment on the city-dwellers, who seemed to have forgotten where the food on their plates came from. Popular anger against urban elites was made acute by a financial crash in 1893, which spread from the banking sector to the wider economy.

A technological revolution was also well underway. Railways, steamships, telegraphs, electric light would all bring enormous benefits over the long term but they also meant short-term disruption and disquiet about the future. Old ways of working were being destroyed as fast as new jobs were being created. The immediate benefits were very unevenly distributed. Some investors made enormous fortunes, while most continued to see their incomes fall. Many people came to believe that elected politicians were in the pocket of special interests. Immigrants – particularly Jews – fell under widespread suspicion.

In the United States, a populist captured the presidential nomination of one of the two main parties. William Jennings Bryan did not win the general election for the Democrats in 1896, but his campaign bore all the hallmarks of future populist assaults on the White House. His style was high-energy, his methods were unconventional and he viewed the political establishment of his own party as the enemy. Bryan bypassed the mainstream media when possible, relying on face-to-face encounters, local news and his own pamphleteering, which often played fast and loose with the facts. He rejected the authority of economic experts, whom he accused of being part of the financial conspiracy that had ensnared ordinary Americans. He blamed foreigners – particularly bankers in the City of London with names like Rothschild – for their plight. If he won, he promised to put the interests of American farmers first.

The breakdown of trust in democratic institutions was not confined to the United States. The 1890s in France were also a time of epic conspiracy theories. The Dreyfus Affair, which started in 1894 with an accusation of treason against an individual officer in the French army, had spread its tentacles by the end of the decade to engulf and then divide the entire French state. Both sides – the supporters and the accusers of Dreyfus – saw in the other a vast, complex plot to destroy the republic, involving Jews and Catholics, German and British agents, communists and bankers. Elected governments were made and broken by these conspiracy theories. French democracy looked to be in danger of collapse. Civil war was a real possibility.

Yet the great populist wave of the late nineteenth century eventually broke. Democracy survived in both France and the United States. Bryan ran three times for the presidency without ever achieving it. The next Democrat to reach the White House in 1913 was Woodrow Wilson, a leading political scientist, former president of Princeton University and unequivocal representative of the expert classes. Dreyfus was exonerated in 1906, after years of disputed inquiries and false dawns. By that point there was still no consensus about where the true conspiracies lay. But that had become the secondary issue. There was finally agreement that enough was enough: French politics had to move on. The military must be put back in its place. There would be no coup.

Are there lessons from this period for today about how to break the spell of populist mistrust of democratic institutions? Early twentieth-century democracy ultimately got an enormous injection of energy from the populist challenge. Elected politicians were forced to confront public anger and find ways to assimilate it back into the mainstream. The age of conspiracy theories was followed by a great age of reform.[27]

In the US, Theodore Roosevelt embarked on his trust-busting campaigns, which used the power of the federal government to break up the big monopolies in oil, steel and banking. He believed that progressive reform was the only thing that could hold democracy together in the face of populist fury. In France, socialists joined the government for the first time and early steps were taken towards the creation of a modern welfare state. In Britain, which had also felt intimations of the populist threat, the modern Labour Party emerged as a political force. The Liberal Party began its own programme of political reform, which included a decisive confrontation with the House of Lords. In the places where democracy had laid down roots, it emerged strengthened by the populist crisis.

However, there is one crucial difference between then and now. Early twentieth-century democracy was young. It had put down roots but it had barely grown. It existed in only a few places and, where it did, it was still incomplete. In Britain, France and the US large sections of the population were denied the vote, including almost all women. In none of those countries did the nation state provide even basic services for many of its citizens. Insurance, healthcare and education were all haphazardly supplied by patchwork arrangements of local, private and charitable providers. Taxes were minimal by today's standards – the top rate of income tax was well below 10 per cent in all of the world's leading democracies in 1900. Levels of public debt were also kept to a minimum. A balanced budget was an article of faith. Politics played little positive role in most citizens' lives. Where they encountered the power of the state, it was largely as something foreign to their everyday experience.

That is what gave a new generation of democratic politicians their chance. They could not prove whether the endless accusations of conspiracy and counter-conspiracy were real. No one can do that. Conspiracy theories are a swamp in which everyone ends up getting drowned. But mainstream politicians could still try to prove that democracy was real. They could tap its untapped potential. It is not clear whether this remains possible today.

Early twentieth-century democratic reformers were able to take advantage of the enormous slack in the system. There was room to grow the franchise, to grow the debt, to grow the power of national government, to grow the tax base, to grow the party system, to grow the labour movement, to grow the public's sense of trust in the state. There was room to grow democracy. None of this was easy because politics never is. It required politicians of great talent and verve, like Roosevelt and Wilson in the US, David Lloyd George in Britain, Jean Jaurès and Georges Clemenceau in France. Populist anger did not disappear, and some of it morphed into even more mistrustful and malign movements that would come close to destroying democracy a generation later. In this period of history, populism could turn into fascism as well as social democracy. Conspiracy theories, in the wrong hands, can unleash a terrible vengeance. But in the US, Britain and even France that did not happen.

Today, there is no equivalent slack in the system. Democracy is no longer young. It lacks the heady sense that existed a century ago of vast, unfulfilled potential.

The battles to expand the franchise have been largely fought and won. The state bears the burden of the huge range of public services that it is expected to provide. Levels of debt, both public and private, are high. Taxes could be higher – they have been higher at periods over the past hundred years – but the popular appetite for paying more is very limited. The current populist backlash in the established democracies is happening in places that have been doing their best with democracy for a while. People are angry with institutions that are unresponsive, not because they are underdeveloped but because they are tired.

This makes breaking the cycle of suspicion much more difficult. Democracy is not working well – if it were, there would be no populist backlash. But attempts to make it work better focus on what we feel we have lost rather than on what we have never even tried. Political arguments revolve around ideas of recovery and rescue – of the welfare state, the constitution, the economy, our security, our freedom. Each side wants to recapture something that has been taken away. This helps to feed the conspiracist mindset. The temptation is to blame the other side for what has been lost – they stole it! The Democrats stole constitutional freedoms! The Republicans stole minority rights! Europe stole British sovereignty! Brexiteers stole workers' rights! All of these accusations are dressed up as rescuing democracy. Trying something new can be a shared democratic experience. Rescuing something that has been lost is partial – the losers look for someone else to blame.

Of course, there are still new things that could be tried. In later chapters I will explore what they might be and how democracy might yet be changed into something that works better. But, for now, what we call democracy looks exhausted in the places where it has the deepest roots. Is there a cure? The history of American democracy shows that at points in the past where it has appeared to be stuck in a rut, the campaign to extend basic democratic rights helped to breathe new life into it. It happened in the 1860s, with the emancipation of slaves; in the early twentieth century, with the enfranchisement of women and the legal protection of labour; in the 1950s and 1960s, with the civil rights movement.

That struggle is not over. There have been recent victories and there are fights yet to be won. Gay rights and the legalisation of gay marriage is one such victory. The ongoing struggle for transgender recognition is another such fight. Yet it is inevitable that as democracy matures, the space for the big battles over the franchise and democratic rights shrinks. The battleground becomes fragmented. Those who remain disenfranchised are on the margins, which means that the case for their liberation can be overtaken by a narrative that says the majority is being sold out for the sake of the few. That is happening today. Identity politics is fuel to the fire of populist frustrations. In 2016 some Republican politicians got as much mileage out of stories about transgender bathrooms as Trump did out of pillorying Hillary Clinton's ties to Wall Street. Common cause is much harder to find than it once was.

The other big difference between then and now is the decline in violence. The turn of the twentieth century was, by contemporary standards, a very violent time. During the 1890s there were more than 2,000 lynchings in the United States. Strikes were routinely broken up with bullets fired by federal and state troops. The Pullman Railroad strike of 1894 was put down by US marshals who killed thirty of the strikers in the process. Race riots were commonplace. In 1898 white supremacists murdered up to sixty black citizens of Wilmington, North Carolina, and drove many others to leave the city. This was ethnic cleansing. Domestic terrorism was widespread. William McKinley, the man who defeated Bryan in the presidential elections of 1896 and 1900, was assassinated by an anarchist in 1901. It sparked an enormous witch-hunt. The last great populist revolt took place against a backdrop of semi-routine political killing.

Contemporary politics is nowhere near as violent. It can sometimes appear more violent, but that is simply a function of how information is now shared and spread. Acts of violence, above all acts of terrorism, are immediately visible in the age of social media: we get to see them taking place in real time. We encounter the violence that happens to others much more directly than we once did. As a result, the secondary experience of violence is now widely shared. But the primary experience of being a victim of violence is rarer than it has ever been. The chances of experiencing violence first hand are lower today than at any point in the past hundred years. For some groups of Americans, particularly for young African-American men, the threat of being a victim of violence remains very real, including at the hands of the state. Yet their experiences are not the ones driving contemporary populism. Donald Trump's talk of the 'carnage' of American life in his inaugural address tapped into these two facts: his supporters see more of it but undergo less of it. That is what helps to fuel the paranoia. The things we only know about second-hand are the things we tend to fear the most.

What the early twenty-first century still has in common with the early twentieth century is the fourth of the conditions I listed as a precondition for the rise of populism: the absence of war. Political violence in an age of populism, no matter how much or how little of it there is, remains localised, piecemeal, sporadic and opportunistic. It is not a collective national experience. Populism feeds off the absence of war because it disputes the idea that democracy is still a genuinely collective experience. That case is much harder to make when the nation is at war. Then the reality of the situation is difficult to avoid: for better or for worse, the people and the elites are in it together.

Certain kinds of wars only provide an ersatz version of a collective national experience. In the late 1890s the US embarked on a war with Spain in various imperial outposts, including Cuba and the Philippines. National feeling was stoked up by a jingoistic press. It did not long survive the end of the conflict because the unity it supplied was superficial, feeding off the production of fake news in the yellow press. The Boer War fought by the British state at the dawn of the twentieth century produced short outbursts of collective national fervour, but in the end the conflict did more to divide the nation than to unite it. The same was true of the Iraq War of 2003, and the ongoing war in Afghanistan. Imperialist adventures do not bring nations together for long. They provide the scope for yet more conspiracy theories because they fuel the idea that the people have been conned.

Wars of national survival are different. In the end, the story of how democracy tamed populism in the first decades of the twentieth century has two parts, both necessary, neither sufficient. One is democratic reform. The other is world war. At this point the parallels between one hundred years ago and today become much less reassuring.

No matter what politicians like Wilson, Clemenceau and Lloyd George were able to achieve before 1914

– and in each case, it was substantial – it was nothing compared to what they were able to do in the era of total war. Fighting wars that needed the full commitment of the entire population required a fuller commitment to democracy to justify the effort. The First World War finally brought about the mass political enfranchisement of women as well as men in Britain and the US. The Second World War delivered it in France, and in other new democracies around the world, including India. The modern welfare state in Britain was a product of the experience of war. Healthy citizens and full employment were necessary to prosecute conflicts that depended on the mobilisation of the national workforce.

In the US the Great Depression triggered a national experiment with political and economic reforms under the terms of the New Deal; but it was the war with fascism that sealed the deal and cemented the power of the federal government to provide for the nation's welfare. This included a far wider distribution of educational benefits, through the GI Bill, which provided funding for returning soldiers to go to college. Likewise, the great social democratic projects of post-Second World War Europe were only made possible by the destruction and desperation that the war had inflicted. An old political science slogan says that states make war and war makes states. Democracy is not an exception to that. Democracies make wars and wars make democracies. This sometimes gets obscured by another slogan of political science, which states that democracies don't go to war with each other. Even if this were true, there have always been enough militant non-democracies to go around.

Military conflicts between democratic and non-democratic states remain a feature of contemporary politics. But the prospect of total war in the twenty-first century has become more or less unthinkable, because the destructive capacity of the leading states is too great to allow it. A total war would be a total disaster. In the absence of wars of national survival we are left with the ersatz kind, which increase rather than undercut public suspicion of democracy. War has become a feature of 'spectator democracy': it is part of the show. It has also become a zone of conspiracy theories.

In the twenty-first century, most citizens do not share the burdens of these wars directly. They are fought at one remove, by drones and special forces, and are paid for indirectly out of public debt and general taxation. They are not a collective experience, except very intermittently, when the news commands our attention. Military conflict does not unite the nation. It divides it between those places where military service is the norm and those where it is almost unheard of. Each mistrusts the other. The unequal experience of warfare has become one of the fault lines of democratic life.

I am not saying that we need total wars to revive democracy. That would be madness. Nor am I saying that the trouble with peace is that it produces conspiracy theories. That would be ridiculous. Having to live with conspiracy theories is a price worth paying for peace. Conspiracy theories are not the real threat anyway – they are only the symptoms of what's gone wrong with democracy. The real difficulty is that it is hard to know how to tackle the causes of populism in the absence of collective encounters with violence.

The third of the conditions I listed as a driver of populism was rising inequality. This has been a persistent problem in modern democratic societies. It is certainly a problem today: Western democracies are reaching levels of inequality in both income and wealth that have not been seen since the end of the nineteenth century, the last great 'gilded age'. Thomas Piketty's *Capital in the Twenty-First Century* (2014) describes the inexorable tendency for inequality to rise over the long history of capitalism, which overlaps with the history of democracy.[28] That trend was reversed during the twentieth century, but even then only as a consequence of the collective experience of war. The violence and destruction of the period between 1914 and 1945 was appalling. But it created the conditions through which rising inequality could be brought under control.

It is true, as Piketty notes, that the democratic reforms that preceded the First World War made some inroads against the advance of inequality. Yet we do not know how far that process would have gone, or if it would ever have gone far enough, because war intervened before the experiment could be completed. Similarly, we do not know whether the New Deal would have been enough to rescue American democracy without war, because war came and made the question redundant. We do not have a historical answer to the question of how to tackle inequality that does not involve large-scale violence. There is no evidence that democracy alone can do it.

The ancient historian Walter Scheidel goes further. In his 2017 book *The Great Leveler* he argues that no society in human history has managed to redress rising inequality without the intervention of large-scale violence.[29] It does not have to take the form of war. Violent revolution, natural disaster, epidemic and plague are all sufficient. They do not need to do their work by breeding forms of social solidarity, as wars of national survival can do. It is enough that the collective experience of violence is sufficiently widespread to ensure that all suffer relatively equally. A calamity that wipes out the property and lives of the rich as effectively as those of the poor will make for a more equal society. It will also be hell on earth.

What does this mean for the future prospects of democracy? The most successful democracies are the ones that have managed to limit violence, ensure against disaster and protect the peaceful lives of their citizens. As a result, inequality has slipped free from the democratic grip in which it was once held. When the political order created in the aftermath of the Second World War broke down at the end of the 1970s, inequality started to rise again. The period since then has seen the continued decline of violence and the continued rise of inequality. The two go together. Both processes accelerated after the end of the Cold War. Then, following the financial crash of 2008, the conditions for a populist backlash against inequality were in place. It became possible to see just how unequal our societies had become, especially once it was clear that the rich would not be punished for the crisis. But these are not the same as the conditions for tackling inequality, which requires more than just a populist revolt. There have been some piecemeal reforms, as there were in 1914. The Obama administration made small inroads into rising inequality. We do not know how far that process would have gone because the Trump presidency intervened.

In democracy we now have a political system that can suppress the causes of violence without being able to address the problems that outbreaks of violence served to resolve in the past. Minor progress is possible. Big progress is elusive, and always liable to be derailed by the backlash small progress provokes. We may be stuck.

This problem of violence and inequality is a large-scale version of the problem of democracy and coups. The violent overthrow of a democracy establishes the conditions under which democracy can be defended: it clarifies the situation. Without that prospect, democracy simply persists and the frustrations that people increasingly feel with it get channelled into forms of mutual mistrust. Ours are not the first democracies in history to get stuck in a rut of conspiracy theories and fake news. But ours are the first with no obvious way out. Reform is possible but it may not be sufficient. Violence is impossible but it may be all that works. Democracies have become very good at solving one problem – violence – that has in the past been a precondition for solving the other – inequality. We do not know what happens next. One possibility is that things carry on as they are. Democracy does not collapse into violence. It simply continues its drift into cranky obsolescence.

Many democracies around the world today still have room to grow and mature. India's democracy is relatively young and it is possible to imagine the scope for reforms that would make it real for hundreds of millions of citizens who have yet fully to feel its benefits. In some parts of the world, including Africa, democracy has barely got going at all. There, political reform can still tap into enormous, unfulfilled potential. The twenty-first century may see a whole series of successful experiments in how far democracy can go towards tackling endemic mistrust and division without falling back into violence.

However, the price of being able to grow is the risk of succumbing to coups, armed takeovers and collapse. The real possibility of democratic failure is one of the preconditions for democratic success. That was true for Western democracy during the twentieth century. But it is no longer true for many well-established democracies today. As a result, the twenty-first century may also see a series of experiments in how long democracy can last in the absence of any agreement about whether it is working or not. Those experiments have no obvious endpoint. But they cannot continue for ever.

A real catastrophe would bring the experiment to an end. But it would also make the experiment pointless. In the twenty-first century the sort of empirical test that could resolve to everyone's satisfaction whether democracy is still working may be the sort of test that no democracy could survive. Waiting for the calamity that settles the issue might mean waiting for the world to end. That is the subject of the next chapter.

2

Catastrophe!

Everywhere was the shadow of death. The farmers told of much illness among their families. In the town the doctors were becoming more and more puzzled by new kinds of sickness that had appeared among their patients. There had been several sudden and unexplained deaths, not only among the adults but also among the children, who would be stricken while they were at play, and would die within a few hours. And there was a strange stillness. The birds, for example – where had they gone?

... The roadsides were lined with brown and withered vegetation, and were silent, too, deserted by all living things. Even the streams were lifeless. Anglers no longer visited them, for all the fish had died. In the gutters and under the eaves, and between the shingles of the roofs, a few patches of white granular powder could be seen; some weeks earlier this powder had been dropped, like snow, upon the roofs and the lawns, the fields and the streams. No witchcraft, no enemy action had snuffed out life in this stricken world. The people had done it themselves.[30]

These are the opening lines to Rachel Carson's 'Silent Spring', first published in the *New Yorker* in June

1962. She is describing a fictional community afflicted by a series of real events. Each of the disasters she lists has happened somewhere, just not all in the same place at the same time. On the face of it, Carson's picture of a society slowly killing itself has got very little to do with the fate of democracy. She is talking about an environmental calamity, not a political one. Yet this is a vision of how democracy might end, too. Her imagined community exists in America, a democratic society. If life ends, democracy ends. And, as Carson says, the disaster was not visited on the community from the outside. 'The people had done it themselves.'

'Silent Spring' was the second of three book-length articles published in the *New Yorker* in the decades after the end of the Second World War that profoundly influenced how we imagine the apocalypse. The first was John Hersey's 'Hiroshima', which appeared in August 1946. It described the experience of nuclear warfare from the perspective of its victims.

> From the mound, Mr Tanimoto saw an astonishing panorama. Not just a patch of Koi, as he had expected, but as much of Hiroshima as he could see was giving off a thick, dreadful miasma. Clumps of smoke, near and far, began to push up through the general dust. He wondered how such extensive damage could have been dealt out of a silent sky … Houses nearby were burning, and when huge drops of water the size of marbles began to fall, he half thought they must be coming from the hoses of firemen fighting the blazes. (They were actually drops of condensed moisture, falling from the turbulent tower of dust, heat and fission fragments that had risen miles into the sky above Hiroshima.)[31]

Hersey's account, based on eyewitness testimony, helped to persuade his readers that nuclear weapons were not simply a means of cowing the enemy into submission. They were a gateway into hell.

The third end-of-times piece was Hannah Arendt's 'Eichmann in Jerusalem', which the *New Yorker* published in four parts over consecutive weeks, beginning in mid-February 1963.[32] Arendt wanted to help her readers to understand how a mousy man in tortoiseshell spectacles could be responsible for the destruction of an entire people. She wanted to understand it herself. She coined a phrase that became the watchword for her thesis: 'the banality of evil'. Adolf Eichmann was not some outlandish monster. He was an unimaginative man incapable of independent thought. That made him capable of monstrous cruelty when the occasion arose. Arendt did not imply that there was an Eichmann in each of us – we are not all latent Nazis. But there are Eichmanns in every society, including our own. In normal times they might work in mundane administrative jobs that suit their lack of imagination. What makes them so dangerous is that they cannot resist when a truly terrible idea comes along. The agents of destruction are not marked out from the rest of the population. They are already among us.

These are the ways modern civilisation could destroy itself. It could blow itself apart with weapons of mass destruction. It could kill itself by fatally poisoning its environment. Or it could allow itself to be infected by evil, which its mindless administrative structures spread through the system, aided by faceless bureaucrats.

In none of these cases is democracy the prime culprit. Hersey did not think that the American people had elected to unleash the horrors of Hiroshima. No one had given them the choice. Truman, who inherited the presidency when Roosevelt died in office in 1945, made a secret decision to use a weapon that had been developed through a secret programme. He only informed the American public about it afterwards. Hersey wanted the American people to understand what had been done in their name. The question was not whether a democratic society would embrace nuclear apocalypse: nobody in their right mind would vote for that. It was whether a democratic society still had the power to stop it.

Carson did not believe that anyone had voted for the destruction of the environment. The overuse of pesticides was not something that was on the ballot. The people had done it by their inattention. They had failed to notice what was taking place all around them. Arendt did not argue that the Holocaust was an active choice by German citizens. Germans had been living in a totalitarian dictatorship that deliberately set out to warp their minds. But Eichmann's terrible example showed how the warping went with the flow of modern bureaucratic methods. Democracies have bureaucracies, too.

Hersey, Carson and Arendt were each, in their different ways, using catastrophe as a means of consciousness-raising. They wanted to describe truly appalling events and scenarios to get their readers to think about the worst that could happen. No one really wants the world to end. The question is whether we will notice what we are doing to end it before it is too late. In the middle of the twentieth century it was hoped that the idea of catastrophe could have a galvanising effect on democratic politics. It would wake people up to the dangers they were running. The fate of democracy may depend on whether that is still true any more.

Catastrophic failures of this kind are very different from coups. When a coup happens it is a disaster for democracy, but life goes on. Society survives. What Eichmann helped inflict on the world was different. It was an existential calamity. It came close to destroying everything of value. For Arendt, the ultimate question posed by modern politics – of which Eichmann was still a frightful representative – was what it would take for 'this planet to remain a fit place for human habitation'. [33] That goes well beyond ensuring the survival of a particular type of political regime. It is about preserving the purpose of human existence.

The trouble with thinking in these terms is that it is hard to keep a sense of perspective. The prospect of catastrophe could easily marginalise the fate of democracy. It might be expendable. After all, democracy can die without everything else perishing as well. Greek society survived the death of Greek democracy. At the same time, we could save democracy and destroy the world. The existential dilemma that Trump might yet pose for his military chiefs is a version of this problem. According to the rules of the American nuclear state, the president must be allowed the sole decision about the use of ultimate force. He could spark a global cataclysm without anyone having the power to stop him. The existence of nuclear weapons gives him that capacity and the Atomic Energy Act of 1946 – which was designed to preserve democracy from trigger-happy generals – enshrines it in law. To save the republic its commander-in-chief is empowered to kill it.

On the other hand, catastrophising won't work as an exercise in consciousness-raising if it makes democracy irrelevant. People need to believe that what they do still matters. Otherwise they are liable to feel powerless. The challenge for anyone wanting to scare people into action is not to scare them into inaction instead. If democracy is just a sideshow, then democratic citizens are bound to feel sidelined. They might drift off again.

Arendt argued that twentieth-century democracy had a form of mindlessness built into it. The creation of modern democracy required the construction of a large administrative apparatus that operates mechanically, according to its own rules and regulations. In this system, technical expertise gets prioritised over human values. Ancient democracy was different. It was real people power. The great danger of modern democracy is that it gets detached from meaningful human input and acquires an artificial life of its own. Human beings still make the key decisions, but they do so without creative insight. They go through the motions. Or they lash out on impulse. What Arendt learned from studying Eichmann was that going through the motions opens the door to our most destructive impulses. We stop thinking for ourselves.

Mindlessness is what links environmental catastrophe, nuclear war and genocidal oblivion. This mindlessness can take different forms. It could be a kind of distraction – while we are busy enjoying ourselves we fail to notice that we are destroying the habitat on which our future depends. It could be a kind of hyperattentiveness – nuclear deterrence gets turned into a technical game of tit-for-tat advantage that loses sight of the risks we run if it all goes wrong. Or it could just be unthinking obedience to a disastrous course of action that we go along with because that's what everyone else is doing. In each case, we need something to break the spell.

Is democracy that something? Or has democracy become the spell?

The threat of environmental disaster today is greater than it was in 1962. Yet it has strangely lost something of its galvanising power – the shadow of death has spread and it has receded at the same time.

The primary danger that Carson highlighted was the mindless use of pesticides like DDT, which she argued came with poorly understood risks that vastly outweighed the benefits. She was mocked by the manufacturers of these chemicals, who painted her as an unthinking enemy of progress. In October 1962, Monsanto, the industrial giant now best known for the development of GM crops, published a parody of *Silent Spring* called 'The Desolate Year':

> Quietly, then, the desolate year began. Not many people seemed aware of the danger. After all, in the winter, hardly a housefly was about. What could a few bugs do, here and there? How could the good life depend on something so seemingly trivial as bug spray? Where were the bugs, anyway?
>
> The bugs were everywhere. Unseen. Unheard. Unbelievably universal. On or under every square foot of land, every square yard, every acre and county and state and region in the entire sweep of the United States. In every home and barn and apartment house and chicken coop, and in their timbers and foundations and furnishings. Beneath the ground, beneath the waters, on and in limbs and twigs and stalks, inside trees and animals and other insects – and yes, inside man.[34]

A series of calamities unfold, as the bugs eat all the food and ravage the land. Monsanto pointed out that, although the scenario was fictional, all these things had once happened somewhere in America – before the invention of pesticides.

Carson won the argument. Her claims came to the attention of President Kennedy, who referred the matter to a Presidential Science Advisory Committee on pesticides in 1963. Their report found that Carson's warnings were largely sound. Pesticides were building up serious risks to human health and causing long-term environmental damage. Regulation was stepped up and the evidence concerning harms and benefits was subject to regular government review. Ten years later the use of DDT was banned.

Carson also succeeded in her consciousness-raising efforts. The publication of her book *Silent Spring* was a key moment in the emergence of the environmental movement, which continued to press the case for greater government action. The success of this kind of pressure politics depends on freedom of information, freedom of association and confidence in the rule of law. It is a largely democratic phenomenon. Polluters can be held to account under those conditions.

Over the following decades the established democracies developed a track record for dealing with contamination of the environment that was far better than any rival system of government. Pollution tended to be much worse under autocratic regimes. The acrid air that hung over much of eastern Europe during the communist era was testament to that. Democracies have two big advantages in dealing with environmental dangers. One is the effective power of pressure groups, which can raise inconvenient truths. The second is market economies, which can experiment with alternative solutions. Pesticides weren't banned altogether after the publication of *Silent Spring*. Only a few were. Most became more effective, as well as safer. The innovators and the lobbyists tend to mistrust each other, as Monsanto and Carson did in 1962. In a healthy democracy this mistrust is productive: each spurs the other to action.

Today that democratic advantage is wearing thin. Air pollution is a huge problem in many Chinese cities. But it is just as bad, if not worse, in democratic India. Breakneck industrial growth, fuelled by large-scale coal-burning, poisons the atmosphere regardless of regime type. Meanwhile, the federal government in the United

States is backtracking on many of the environmental protections that were Carson's legacy, though some state governments are doing their best to resist. Democracy is starting to look increasingly erratic when it comes to maintaining a fit space for human habitation.

The warnings of catastrophe that Carson managed to register with the US government and the wider public no longer resonate as they did. There are three reasons for this. One is success: there is less to fear once our earlier fears have been dealt with. The greater risk now is complacency. Having seen off one threat, we are tempted to think that any fresh dangers are being exaggerated, forgetting what it was that rescued us first time around. Second, the politics of environmental regulation are much more divisive than they were half a century ago. The economist Paul Krugman has argued that rising inequality is part of the reason why.[35] Concerted action on environmental threats requires some agreement on the value of public goods. A more unequal society makes that agreement harder to achieve because the costs and benefits are much less equitably distributed. In 1970, during President Nixon's first term, the Clean Air Act passed the Senate by a vote of 73–0. Unanimity on any issue, above all on an environmental one, is almost unimaginable in the current political climate. The third reason for the change is that Carson's vision of the worst that can happen has long been superseded by another kind of threat. The space for worrying about environmental disaster is now fully occupied by the idea of climate change. It is a bigger danger than pesticides. But it does not threaten us in the same way.

This is not for want of writers trying to scare us into action. Contemporary fiction is full of visions of a rapidly warming world that more than match the horror of Carson's dystopia: parched landscapes, marauding survivors, collapsed social institutions and an explosion of violence are what await us. But this is in an imagined future. Carson set out to describe what was already happening. The coming catastrophe of climate change is still only a whisper in many people's lived experience. That may be starting to change in the coastal regions of the southern United States. It is also being felt in some of the poorest parts of the world, where the effects of climate change are more immediately experienced. But it is not true everywhere. It was part of Carson's genius to convey a sense of universal threat. It could happen anywhere. By contrast, climate change divides more than it unites us.

Contemporary journalism has tried to emulate Carson and capture the harm that climate change has already caused, especially in the developing world, where resources are more scarce and people more vulnerable. But for the inhabitants of better-off regions these descriptions lack the immediacy and specificity of Carson's account. They also lack the novelty. We have become relatively inured to apocalyptic descriptions of our future because we have been exposed to so many of them. There is a distinct sense of apocalypse fatigue.

The result is that fears of climate change have not produced the same effect that fears about pesticides did for an earlier generation. The threat of global warming is more ubiquitous, more diffuse and more uncertain. It does not have the requisite bite. Instead of breaking the spell of suspicion and conspiracy, it has reinforced it. Many of the most intractable contemporary conspiracy theories concern climate change. It frequently gets described as a hoax. The reasoning goes like this: the secret elites who want to establish world government need a problem that requires collective action on a global scale to justify their ambitions. Climate change is such a problem. Therefore the secret elites must have invented it and bought off the scientists. This is the answer you get once the primary question in politics has become: who benefits?

Ask who benefits from these attempts to discredit the science of climate change and you get an equally clear answer: the fossil fuel industry. Conspiracy theories on one side are matched by conspiracy theories on the other. There are real conspiracies, too: ExxonMobil has funded much of the research that casts doubt on the scientific consensus. But suspicion breeds suspicion, so that environmentalists too often reach for conspiratorial explanations as the default explanation for why their cause is not making more progress. This breakdown of trust has become self-reinforcing rather than self-correcting. The furious arguments about who is conning whom over climate change are poisoning democracy.

They are also fuelling executive aggrandisement. This is the route Obama took, after he found it impossible to get environmental legislation through Congress (it is sobering to think that Nixon could readily do what Obama couldn't). As a political solution, relying on executive orders to address this problem has two big flaws. First, what an executive does, an executive can overturn. Obama's legacy on climate has proved much easier to undo than his legacy on healthcare because Trump could rescind his predecessor's executive orders simply by signing some of his own. Second, the attempt to avoid a partisan legislature makes the partisanship worse. If no one is trying to strike a deal, no one has anything to lose by digging in. Democratic politics is always damaged by the attempt to get round it.

It is no longer possible to argue that what is needed is more consciousness raising. When it comes to climate change the public is not ignorant of the risks. They have been forced down our throats for years. Carson wanted to let an oblivious world know about the dangers it was running in its neglect of long-term environmental damage. We already know what we are doing. It's just that many of us don't want to know.

Instead, most of the consciousness raising is coming from the other side. The most passionate advocates in the arena of climate politics are the deniers, who see it as a liberal plot. There is a lot of frenetic democratic energy being devoted to challenging the reality of climate change. It is deeply unproductive. As Arendt implied, modern politics makes it possible to be in a manic state and to be in a trance at the same time. When it comes to climate change, democracy increasingly looks like the spell, not the cure. The arrival of Trump in the White House, and his professed wish to take the United States out of the Paris climate accord (leaving the country in a minority of one) has redirected some of the political energy against the doubters. But it has done nothing to dispel the miasma of mistrust.

If and when the fictions of environmental disaster turn to fact, democratic politics can be expected to snap out of it. That is one of democracy's strengths: chaos and violence bring out the best in it. Environmental politics was more tractable in the 1960s because the leading democracies were still living with the legacy of a world war that had come close to destroying everything. The problem now is that, unlike then, when we were poisoning the rivers and killing the birds out of the sky, the decisive evidence of what we have done looks like coming too late. When we finally want to know, the knowledge will turn out to have been there all along. At that point, it may be of little help.

What about the fear of nuclear apocalypse? Where do we now stand in relation to that? Hersey's book

Hiroshima remains widely read, especially by school-children. His description of what happens when a nuclear weapon is detonated over a large urban area has never been bettered because the experience has never been repeated – bar once, a few days later in Nagasaki. This horror story is less dated than Carson's since we have nothing to compare it with. It retains a visceral immediacy. But in another sense it is even more remote. It is over seventy years since the world was forced to think about what nuclear warfare does to human habitation in practice. In that time the danger of nuclear conflict has greatly increased, as the weapons have become much more powerful and more widely distributed. But the fear we have of them has lost much of its power to spur us into action. It is still terrifying but it is theoretical. It is communicated to us through the technical warnings of informed elites. It is not grounded in experience.

During the Cold War the threat of all-out nuclear war was real enough to generate widespread popular resistance. The anti-nuclear lobby could match the envir-onmental movement for scale and scope. In the UK the Campaign for Nuclear Disarmament (CND) had more than two million members at its peak, making it one of the largest civil society organisations in Europe. Mass participation coincided with the ratcheting up of nuclear tensions between the superpowers – it happened in the early 1960s, at the time of the Cuban Missile Crisis, and again in the early 1980s, when the Reagan administration was trying to win the arms race. It hasn't happened since.

Today, CND is a shell of what it was, with only a few thousand members and almost no public profile. The irony is that one of its most committed supporters, Jeremy Corbyn, was elected leader of the Labour Party in

2015 and could yet find himself as British prime minister. Nuclear disarmament still animates Corbyn, but it barely resonates with his supporters from a younger generation, who have little memory of the Cold War. Corbyn was obliged to run in the 2017 British general election on a manifesto that committed the UK to retaining its Trident nuclear deterrent. Abolishing nuclear weapons was much lower down Labour's order of priorities than abolishing student tuition fees. Corbyn may yet change the party's official position on Trident, but if he does, it will be as a sop to his ideological heritage, not to the pressure of public opinion. Nuclear disarmament has lost its bite as a popular cause.

Instead, it has been adopted by an elite group of unelected power-brokers and turned into an international governance issue. The double irony is that, while Corbyn is stuck with the bomb, Henry Kissinger wants to get rid of it. The strongest push for nuclear disarmament in recent years has come from a group of four former US policy chiefs – Kissinger, George Shultz, William Perry and Sam Nunn – 'the four horsemen of the nuclear apocalypse', as *Time* magazine dubbed them.[36] The first two had been Secretaries of State; Perry was once Secretary of Defense; only Nunn, a former Senator, has ever been elected to anything. All four were among the exponents of the Cold War strategy that saw nuclear weapons as the guarantors of peace. With the Cold War over, they came to view nuclear weapons as the greatest threat to international security and wished to see them abolished. Their case is persuasive. But its democratic credentials are practically non-existent. Nuclear disarmament has been turned into another problem for the grown-ups in the room to resolve.

At the height of the Cold War, nuclear weapons were the drivers of political paranoia. Stanley Kubrick's 1964 masterpiece *Dr Strangelove or: How I Learned to Stop Worrying and Love the Bomb* is the great cinematic representation of the paranoid style in American politics. It satirised the world of conspiracy theories and it helped to fuel them. The inevitable secrecy of the nuclear state made it ripe for the wildest kinds of suspicion – in the upside-down universe of Mutually Assured Destruction (MAD) nothing was too crazy to be believable. Today, though we live in an age when conspiracy theories are everywhere, few of them concern nuclear weapons. The paranoia has spread its wings and moved on. Kissinger, once the pre-eminent symbol of the sinister underside of American democracy, is now just another has-been on the international conference circuit. When it turned out Kissinger had been advising Trump behind the scenes, most people weren't terrified. They were mildly reassured. That's how things have changed.

The threat of nuclear calamity is an inverted version of the threat posed by climate change. Both are undermined as a political cause by the uncertainty that surrounds them. In the case of climate change the uncertainty concerns the future – though we have intimations of disaster we don't know what will happen or when, which makes it very difficult to find a focal point for political action. With nuclear weapons the uncertainty is about the past – we don't really know how we survived to this point. Was it political skill? Was it luck? The Cold War saw plenty of close brushes with nuclear calamity, of which the public was largely unaware at the time. Planes nearly crashed; military orders got garbled; commanders got drunk. Is the history of our continued peaceful existence just a meaningless pattern of near-misses that could be made redundant at any moment by some terrible accident or design? The next time a nuclear weapon is detonated with human beings in the firing line everything changes. Until that happens – or until nuclear weapons are abolished – nothing really changes. The uncertainty persists.

The irony is that the use of nuclear weapons is now more likely than it was a generation ago. We no longer live in a world of mutually assured destruction. Nuclear warfare could take place without destroying everything. Terrorists may acquire crude versions of nuclear weapons, in which case any taboo against their use would be meaningless. Equally, the super-sophisticated versions now available to the American military may tempt a commander-in-chief to see them as an extension of conventional warfare, capable of tactical precision and contained fall-out. Yet the consequences remain unfathomable. The taboo exists for a reason.

Climate change lacks political grip on our imaginations because it is so incremental. The environmental apocalypse is only ever a creeping catastrophe. We experience it as a rumour. Nuclear catastrophe lacks grip because it is an all-or-nothing phenomenon. There is nothing that can make it real without threatening to make everything else effectively meaningless. It is too huge to grasp. So we cross our fingers and hope that our luck holds.

What, finally, about evil? Are we still sufficiently frightened of that? Trump's election as president has got people worrying about the Nazis once more. We are back to looking at the 1930s for guidance. In 2017 the historian Timothy Snyder published *On Tyranny: Twenty Lessons from the Twentieth Century*, which warned against assuming that the worst couldn't happen again. The lesson of Weimar Germany is that democracy won't save itself by itself. In the end, its democratic credentials left it defenceless against a hostile takeover. Instead, active citizens are needed to save democracy from itself.

Snyder draws on Arendt to make his case. He cites her warnings about a world corroded by conspiracy theories, 'where we are seduced by the notion of hidden realities and dark conspiracies that explain everything'. This marks the beginnings of totalitarianism – 'post-truth', Snyder says, 'is pre-fascism'. He highlights the dangers of simply going with the flow – the mindlessness of conformity. 'Some killed from murderous conviction. But many others who killed were just afraid to stand out. Other forces were at work beside conformism. But without the conformists, the great atrocities would have been impossible.'[37]

Invoking the dark shadow of the Holocaust raises the stakes but it also heightens the risk of crying wolf. Calling conspiracy theories the precursors of totalitarianism ignores the fact that many twenty-first century conspiracy theorists see themselves as the last vanguard against totalitarianism. One of Snyder's rules of resistance is: 'Investigate. Figure things out for yourself.' That is exactly what many of Trump's supporters believe they are doing. They are the non-conformists. They are the ones thinking for themselves. And if Snyder contends that they are deluded fools – because they are simply following the fake news they are being fed online – they would respond that *he* is the conformist. He is the one peddling the laughable liberal stereotype that Trump is a proto-Hitler.

This argument will not be resolved when the true horror finally reveals itself. Twenty-first century democracies like the United States can keep putting that moment off. The wolf will not arrive. If Trump never turns into Hitler – and he won't – then everyone can claim to have been proved right.

In an age of populism, while some anxious defenders of democracy are invoking the banality of evil, others are busy railing against the evil of banality. For many populists, mindless bureaucracy is not at risk of being invaded by a truly terrible idea it is powerless to resist. Instead, mindless bureaucracy *is* the truly terrible idea and the correct democratic response is to resist it. Both sides in populist politics – the populists and the anti-populists – believe they are fighting the good fight to save democracy from itself. The central division of our time is not democracy v. conspiracy theory. It is conspiracy theory v. conspiracy theory in the name of democracy. This is not the 1930s all over again. It is the 1890s, without the prospect of resolution.

Conjuring up the spectre of Hitler runs together two different ways democracy can end. Nazism was the death of democracy in the sense that it killed a democratic political regime – the Weimar Republic – and replaced it with a dictatorship. German society survived, just. Nazism was also a glimpse into the abyss, where everything falls apart. Once Nazism collided with Stalinism, the very worst happened. In 'the bloodlands' of central and eastern Europe, harrowingly described by Snyder in his book of that name, human life effectively lost all meaning.[38]

In the middle of the twentieth century, the death of democracy as a form of politics was the precursor for the possible death of civilisation. But in the twenty-first century, it is the other way around. Democracy survives because very little can now kill it as a form of politics. The death of civilisation might have to come first. Conformists and non-conformists do all they can to keep democracy going, furiously denigrating the efforts of the other side. Meanwhile, the threat of catastrophe hovers over us, untouched.

* * *

IS THERE ANY WAY to think constructively about the end of the world? We can't ignore doomsday scenarios – that would be highly irresponsible. But if we spend too much time worrying about the very worst that could happen, we will not spend enough time on the other things that matter. Like a hypochondriac, we will get preoccupied with death. As a result, our perspective on life could end up seriously skewed.

The problem is that a total catastrophe is not just somewhat worse than a partial catastrophe – it is utterly different. The end of everything trumps everything else. The philosopher Derek Parfit framed the issue like this. Imagine three scenarios:

1. All humans die.
2. 99 per cent of all humans die.
3. No humans die.[39]

The first scenario is exponentially worse than the second, whereas the second is only relatively worse than the third. If we are talking about the preservation of things of fundamental human value, going from a death toll of zero to 99 per cent is not as bad as going from 99 per cent to 100 per cent. It sounds heartless and it is hard to reconcile with the idea that each individual human being has value – in the second scenario, almost everybody dies! But the difference is that in the first scenario, when absolutely everybody dies, there is no hope of recovery and no one left to do the valuing. Everything is lost.

One response to this problem is known as 'the precautionary principle', which states that we need to make a special effort to guard against hard-to-evaluate but potentially catastrophic outcomes. The precautionary principle is often applied to environmental threats. For instance, we don't know how disastrous the effects of unchecked climate change could be – they might be nowhere near as bad as feared or they might pose a real threat to the continued existence of human civilisation. Even if there is only a small chance of the latter – and especially if we really have no idea what sort of chance it is – it is worth taking special precautions. Our inability to be sure about the risks we run is a reason to take action now rather than to delay action until we can be sure. If we act and it was a wasted effort, the costs will be livable with. If we don't act and the worst happens, they won't. This is a version of Pascal's wager, which says that it's never worth taking a chance on eternal damnation.

The precautionary principle has plenty of critics. They point out that it can end up warping our judgement by causing us to downgrade other kinds of hazards. If some exceptional risks stand apart from everything else, then non-exceptional risks may struggle to get taken seriously. That has costs, too. For example, taking pre-emptive action on climate change generates significant risks of its own – it could stifle growth in developing countries, leading to loss of life (economic growth underpins improved healthcare), social unrest and political conflict. Those are survivable outcomes – if they weren't, the human race would hardly have made it this far. But do we really think that even in the very worst-case scenario, climate change will not be survivable by anyone? So long as there are survivors from any catastrophe, then there is no reason to say that it can't be compared to other kinds of risks. Only cases where everything is lost deserve special treatment.

A different terminology has been designed to capture this final distinction. 'Existential risk' refers to events from which there really is no coming back. On the existential score sheet, even the death of all humans does not constitute the ultimate calamity. We might do something worse. We could destroy the planet and end all life on earth. We could go further and destroy the entire universe, were some hubristic physics experiment to go very badly wrong. That would not just put paid to our own existence but to any forms of life that we don't even yet know about. This sounds extremely far-fetched. But if there is even the tiniest prospect that scientists meddling with the laws of physics could roll the universe up into a tiny ball, the theory of existential risk says we must guard against it.

Set against the death of the universe, the death of democracy looks like a trivial concern. Many of those who champion this way of thinking believe that democracy is one of the things we should do everything in our power to preserve from the ashes. It helps make life worth living. But that is different from thinking that democracy is what will preserve us. Existential risk ultimately makes democracy expendable. We have to do whatever it takes. If this is an exercise in consciousness-raising, its targets are scientists, policy-makers, philosophers. It does not really matter who gets to decide what happens next. What matters is what gets decided. Either there is a next, or there isn't.

In the twenty-first century, this means that the landscape of ultimate disaster includes some twentieth-century visions of the apocalypse, but it goes well beyond them. Nuclear holocaust still looms large – were even a small fraction of the thousands of nuclear weapons dotted around the earth to be detonated at the same time, little would be left. Climate change features in the form of potentially 'catastrophic' global warming or cooling – runaway effects and feedback loops could yet see the planet consumed by fire or ice. Bio-engineering is a new existential threat, particularly if it morphs into bio-terrorism. But the most acute contemporary fears concern the unchecked power of new technology. This is the latest version of the apocalypse. We may soon be at risk of unleashing machines that we cannot control.

These machines might be minuscule – a long-standing anxiety about nanotechnology relates to the possible creation of tiny, self-replicating bots that end up consuming the world in grey goo. Alternatively, they could be recognisably like ourselves, but with something important missing. Rapid advances in machine learning have brought forward the possibility of creating devices that mimic human intelligence, without having the sense of perspective that makes us human. Set a task, these machines might destroy everything in their pursuit of it – told to maximise paperclip production, they could drown the world in a sea of paperclips. We could switch them off. But what if there is no off switch? What if the machines control the off switch? What if the machines realise that to prevent us switching them off they have to switch us off instead?

It seems like an indulgence to argue about who voted for what when the killer robots are coming. In the rarefied atmosphere of existential risk, politics barely gets discussed at all. Instead, putative solutions focus on technical fixes – like building off switches that can't be tampered with. Meaningful choices for human beings get reduced to the decisions of the few people who understand how the technology works – they are the ones who need to do the right thing. Only those with the capacity to build these machines have the capacity to stop them. Everyone else is a bystander.

The idea that existential risk sucks the life out of democracy is not entirely new. Some political thinkers believe that democracy came to an end when the atomic bomb came into being. The voters are too fickle; the weapons are too terrible. Special measures will always be needed to keep them apart. On this account, democracy and the destructive power unleashed at Hiroshima cannot co-exist. The Harvard social theorist Elaine Scarry spells out the nature of the choice in her recent book *Thermonuclear Monarchy: Choosing between Democracy and Doom*. 'Nuclear weapons undo governments and undo anything that could be meant by democracy,' she says. 'We had a choice: get rid of nuclear weapons or get rid of Congress and the citizens. We got rid of Congress and the citizens.'[40]

Scarry wants to bring democracy back to life by abolishing the nuclear state. It is not going to happen. There are two reasons why. First, if democracy was killed by nuclear weapons, then democracy is in no position to get rid of them. It will have to be done by the nuclear state itself. The people will be bystanders to their own rescue. Second, even if we get rid of nuclear weapons, there are too many other existential risks that can stymie democracy on their own. As the capacity of human beings to wreak havoc on their habitat increases, nuclear war has lost its special status as the totem of our destructive power. If we couldn't be trusted with the bomb, we can't be trusted with AI either; or with bioengineering; or with the Large Hadron Collider. Nuclear weapons began the age of existential risk but they no longer define it. We might put one genie back in the bottle. We won't put them all back.

Democracy cannot control existential risk. The most it can hope for is to be spared by it. This is how democracy gets treated by the existential risk-management industry: with kid gloves, like some precious object of historic value that might yet turn out to have an incidental use. No one wants to dismiss democracy out of hand. It would be terrible to see it disappear, just as it would be terrible to imagine the Louvre going up in a puff of smoke. So it gets brought along for the existential ride.

Nick Bostrom, a philosopher based at Oxford's Future of Humanity Institute, is a leading exponent of the idea that ordinary risk management is ineffective when it comes to the life-threatening technologies of the twenty-first century. He is particularly concerned by the possible impact of 'super-intelligent' AI machines that operate beyond any human control. He also worries about nuclear war and environmental catastrophe. Bostrom sees the value of democracy. He just does not see it as a priority. It is possible that spreading democracy could help preserve the human race by making peace more likely than war. But spending time on democracy is a risk in itself when there are other, more practical things to be getting on with. 'With limited resources,' Bostrom writes, 'it is crucial to prioritize wisely. A million dollars could currently make a vast difference to the amount of research done on existential risks; the same amount spent on furthering world peace would be like a drop in the ocean.' [41]

At the same time, Bostrom worries that democracy could get in the way of the rescue act. In democratic societies, it is hard to persuade people to focus on the risk of things that haven't happened yet and will probably never happen. Voters tend to prioritise what they know. It may be that everyone's survival depends on taking pre-emptive action against dangers that have yet to manifest themselves. 'Democracies will find it difficult to act decisively before there has been any visible demonstration of what is at stake. Waiting for such a demonstration is decidedly not an option, because it might itself be the end.' [42]

Bostrom is an unusual person, the subject of deep

fascination in parts of the tech industry. A *New Yorker* profile of him in 2016 portrays a man who sees further than other people, and therefore does not always notice what is in front of him. Given the pace of technological change, imagining what life will be like in twenty years' time is formidably difficult for most of us. Bostrom believes we have a duty to think about what life might be like one million years from now. He also has a desire to evade death. As one of his friends puts it: '[Nick's] interest in science was an outgrowing of his understandable desire to live forever, basically.'[43]

The title of the *New Yorker* piece is 'The Doomsday Invention', which echoes the exercises in apocalyptic consciousness-raising that the magazine undertook in the middle of the twentieth century. Yet the tone is completely different. The profile of Bostrom is jaunty, ironic, its author coolly amused by the intellectual ambition of a man 'who believes that his work could dwarf the moral importance of anything else'. There is something quaint about Bostrom's unembarrassed willingness to engage with apparently absurd scenarios. Bostrom's champions have compared his warnings about the catastrophic potential of AI to Carson's 'Silent Spring'. But that is not how he comes across. He is well beyond that. In 'The Doomsday Invention' there is no discussion of politics at all.

So let's go back to nuclear weapons. There is still a puzzle here. If existential risk spells the end of democracy, what happened after Hiroshima?

During the four decades of the Cold War, when the world had to live with the daily threat of destruction, democracy appeared to thrive. This was the great period of democratic uplift: democracy spread, it stabilised and it prospered. It was an era that culminated in Fukuyama's claim that we had arrived at the end of history, with liberal democracy left in possession of the field. Even if we no longer believe that, it is clear that modern democracy had its best years when the nuclear state was also in the ascendant. If nuclear weapons are fatal to democracy, how did democracy manage to live with them so successfully?

Part of the answer is: wishful thinking. The kind of democracy that flourished during the Cold War did not operate at the level of existential choice. It was built on bread-and-butter issues: welfare, jobs, education. The nuclear state, by bearing the weight of the ultimate fate of the world, gave the democratic state room to breathe. Yet the separation was not total. The bomb still found its way into democratic arguments. The vibrant anti-nuclear movements of the early 1960s and the early 1980s showed its power to mobilise large numbers of concerned citizens. Disarmament was sometimes an issue at the polls, and so too was the communist threat. The voters were not oblivious to the risks being run.

Democracy thrived under these conditions because existential questions could be brought down to the level of bread-and-butter politics. The issue at election time was not really the fate of the world. It never is. What counted was how people felt about the politicians who were taking decisions on their behalf, big and small. That is always the basic question of representative democracy: what do we think about *these* people deciding for us? It doesn't matter so much what is at stake. It could be a question of nuclear apocalypse or it could be a question of the price of bread.

In October 1962, between the publication of 'Silent Spring' and 'Eichmann in Jerusalem', the world came as close as it ever has to nuclear catastrophe. During the thirteen days of the Cuban Missile Crisis the two nuclear superpowers looked set to unleash the unimaginable. As the climax approached, with Russian and American ships apparently set on a collision course, the fate of human civilisation hung in the balance. At the last, Kennedy and Khrushchev found a path back from the edge of the abyss, through a mixture of skill and luck. Ten days after that, the American voting public was given the chance to pass a verdict on its epic good fortune in the mid-term elections for Congress. How did they reward the president? Kennedy's Democrats lost seats in both the House of Representatives and the Senate. The issue that was bothering the voters in the places where he was punished at the polling booth: grain prices.

When people have grown frustrated with one set of politicians or another, they make use of whatever tools are to hand. Nuclear politics, like green politics, can be a vehicle for reminding politicians not to take us for granted. That does not mean that democracy is capable of getting a grip on existential threats. It simply means that existential threats are sometimes a good way of kicking politicians where it hurts. Today, when much of the political establishment is committed to taking climate change seriously, rejecting it is a way for people who have had enough to make themselves heard. It is always a mistake to assume that one side in a democratic contest cares about the fate of the planet and the other side doesn't. Both sides care and neither side cares. Both care because no one wants the world to end. Neither cares because this is democracy: what people really care about is who gets to tell them what to do.

The experts don't much like being told what to do either. Conscious that democratic politics risked infecting nuclear strategy with irrationality, an attempt was made during the Cold War to carve out a separate space for existential decision-making. The branch of economics known as 'rational choice theory' was applied to questions of nuclear deterrence. The aim was to ensure that the optimal strategy was pursued at all times. Something as deadly serious as nuclear conflict should be immune from fickle human judgements about who gets to decide what. The best way to achieve that was to treat nuclear deterrence as a kind of game with its own set of rules. This is the approach that *Dr Strangelove* satirises: in order to save the world we must be prepared to destroy it many times over, if that's what the game book of nuclear strategy dictates. It's MAD. But it makes sense in its own terms.

Yet game theory and democracy cannot be kept entirely apart. They bleed into each other. This is partly because democracy has turned out to be useful for playing certain kinds of games. One way to think about nuclear deterrence is as a game of chicken – in which case the best strategy is to appear irrational, so that the other player blinks first. If two cars are driving straight at each other, the one to swerve is likely to have a driver who believes the other driver might be crazy enough not to swerve at all. If American presidents were not wholly free to put nuclear strategy in the hands of the experts, because fickle democratic public opinion wouldn't let them, it could be a strategic advantage. It would make the Russians think twice. Seen from the perspective of game theory, democratic decision-making is often idiotic. But it can be a useful idiot.

At the same time, the game theorists had political ambitions of their own. Once nuclear war had been carved out as a separate space for technical experts to play in, why stop there? If democracy is an idiot, then surely we should try to impose stricter rules on the other areas of political life. The welfare state, the education system and the democratic process itself all looked ripe for an injection of cool, unsentimental, analytical thinking. If everyone were treated as a rational agent, out to maximise his or her advantage, then much of life could potentially be spared from the confusion of democracy.

As a result, the thinking that had found a foothold in the nuclear state started to spread outwards. From the late 1970s democratic politics became infected with game theoretic models of how the economy should work. The messiness of political life was supplanted by the clean lines of perfect competition and efficient markets. These proved remarkably effective so long as the mess of democracy could be kept at bay. Their ascendancy coincided with the period when it was widely believed that not only had history come to an end, but boom and bust was also a thing of the past. Models of how the world should work in theory came to be preferred over models of how it had worked in practice. Eventually, history caught up with the models. Following the financial crash of 2008, the mess of democracy returned with a vengeance. It is still wreaking its revenge today.

If the problem with democracy is that it can turn a nuclear stand-off into bread-and-butter politics, the problem with game theory is that it can turn bread-and-butter politics into a nuclear stand-off. It treats the choices faced by individuals as though they could be modelled in existential terms: I win, you lose and context is irrelevant. It is absurdly clear-cut. Democracy is not. Treating it as though it should be does not bring democracy to heel. It simply adds to the uncertainty.

The lesson of the Cold War and beyond is that democracy can co-exist with existential risk, but not on terms that make sense to either side. Thinking about the end of the world is too much for democracy to cope with, but not enough to kill it off. Democracy persists, unhappily joined to a partner it cannot really tolerate.

This is not the world of Dr Strangelove any more. I have passed time in the company of people who spend their days worrying about existential risk. The researchers into the coming age of intelligent robots, superbugs and planetary destruction are mild-mannered and well-meaning. They have no beef with democracy and when the occasion requires they will pay tribute to its virtues. But they are not really interested in politics. It looks like a distraction from the overriding question of the twenty-first century, which is whether the human race will come out the other side.

What keeps many of these good people awake at night is the nightmare of intelligent machines that run out of our control. This is the ultimate version of the banality of evil: mindless robots chewing up whatever lies in their path. But it is not what Arendt meant by the banality of evil. It has no political dimension. There is no way to wake these machines up, to snap them out of their trance. They are nothing but machines. This is a technical problem, not a political one. We simply have to find the off switch.

Trying to prevent politics from interfering with the project of saving the world is a noble impulse. But it is a mistake. Democracy cannot be contained in its well-tended corner of the garden. So long as it survives it will inevitably spill out from its enclosure. Democracies do not take kindly to being contained. It leaves people feeling that they are being taken for granted. They react badly to having well-meaning experts take the important decisions for them. What do we think about these people being in charge? Soon enough, we will reach for whatever grievances we have to hand.

During the twentieth century many of the worst things that could happen to democracy brought out the best in it – wars, financial crises and other disasters woke people up to the risks they were running. But as existential risks have started to overshadow other kinds of threats, democracy has been weakened. Existential risk brings out the worst in democracy. People power and technical expertise get pulled apart without quite coming apart. Neither gives up hope of bringing the other back into line. They co-exist in an uneasy relationship of semi-estrangement. So long as the worst never happens, it is a chilly marriage that could last for a long time.

THERE IS ONE FURTHER FEAR that haunts the twenty-first century political imagination. It is the fear of inter-connectedness. We have a nagging feeling that our world has become vulnerable to collapse because everything is joined to everything else. If one thing fails, it could all fail. Global systems of finance, energy, communication, health and transportation are joined in ways that no one controls and no one fully understands. Complexity on this scale is fragile because shocks might spread through the system before anyone has time to react. A pandemic could circulate round the globe in a few hours thanks to mass air travel. A crash in one corner of the inter-national financial system could trigger knock-on effects everywhere. A failure in the power supply could bring everything to a grinding halt.

What makes networks frightening is the thought that they could collapse without any warning. There does not need to be human intent involved. A network might simply out. Because there is no single point of control – no off switch – any part of the network could turn out to be the weak link. The strength of networks is what makes them dangerous: no one and nothing is in charge of what happens next.

Contemporary fiction is where these fears come to life. In Cormac McCarthy's *The Road* (2006), the apocalypse is brought on by an event that is unspecified. It takes place somewhere on the distant horizon. All we learn is that there was 'a long shear of light and then a series of low percussions'.[44] It is all we need to know. Something happens and the reverberations leave nothing untouched. The something could be anything. In David Mitchell's *The Bone Clocks* (2014), climate change has caused the planes to fall out of the sky. Communities are cut off from each other because networked communication has failed. We are not told how or why. It does not matter. We recognise that a civilisation like ours might fall apart without anyone fully understanding what caused what. We are vulnerable to forces beyond our power to control. Everything depends on the system – the grid – the network – the web – the machine. It has to keep on working. Until one day it doesn't.[45]

This dread of interconnectedness has been around for a long time. In his short story 'The Machine Stops', written more than a hundred years ago, E. M. Forster conjured up a dystopia fit for the twenty-first century.[46] Forster describes the sterile existence of isolated individuals in a networked world of the future, which is brought to an end when the mechanism on which they all depend ceases to function. These people can only communicate with each other via a form of instant messaging. They have little to share but their fantasies. Their pleasures come at the touch of a button. They have no true experiences of their own. The failure of 'the machine' that rules their lives is death and it is liberation.

Forster believed human beings should 'only connect', not interconnect. The terrible danger of everything being joined to everything else is the loss of any sense of perspective. We have no means of deciding what really matters because nothing is irrelevant and nothing is truly important. There is only one way the story can end, with systemic collapse. We are at the mercy of the things that link us because we have no way of encountering the world unmediated by them. To break free is to break the chain. At that point, it all falls apart.

The current version of this nightmare embraces more than just information networks. We are linked by a shared ecosystem, by complex chains of energy supply, by intertwined financial markets that move faster than human beings can think, by transport systems that run at the edge of full capacity all the time. We know that one mishap can cause gridlock and shutdown. We have all experienced it at some point: waiting at an airport where nothing is working; sitting in a hospital that is over capacity; staring at a blank computer screen that has stopped functioning. We don't know what gridlock or shutdown would mean if it applied to everything all at once. But we can guess.

In these scare stories, there is little or no place for politics. What drives our fears is a sense of powerlessness in the face of complexity. That is why so many contemporary dystopians are uninterested in how we got from here to there. It just happened. The basic questions that animate democracy – what do we want to do? who do we want to do it? where do we want to go next? – are irrelevant if we are waiting for the day when the machine stops.

Images of human beings in the grip of forces they have lost the power to control often portray them as being in a kind of trance. A mechanical, hyper-connected existence is sterile. It can also act as a kind of sedative. We appear to be fully engaged but we do not really see what we are doing. We are only going through the motions.

The idea that we might sleepwalk into disaster is a lesson that historians have drawn from the horrors of the twentieth century. Christopher Clark's *The Sleepwalkers: How Europe Went to War in 1914* (2013) is the definitive contemporary account of the great unintended catastrophe of the modern age: the outbreak of the First World War.[47] No one really sought it. No one understood how to stop it. Nothing was pre-ordained. Contingent choices, shaped by particular circumstances, drove individuals to make what would only emerge in hindsight as catastrophic mistakes. These politicians were not simply in some hypnotic trance, doing what the system demanded of them. They were moving purposefully in their sleep, jerkily incontinent, full of energy and life, oblivious to the wider picture. They were sleepwalking to disaster as gamblers do, blind to their inability to control their fate.

There are echoes of this horror story in contemporary politics. Its shadow is inescapable. If the United States and North Korea were to go to war, it would be because the leading actors were unable to wake up to the risks they were running. The possibility of catastrophic mistakes that only reveal themselves after the event is always with us.

Yet the fear of interconnectedness can also produce the opposite effect. Far from being asleep, many contemporary politicians are permanently alert to the danger of making the mistake from which there is no coming back. They are, if anything, hyper-attentive to the risks they run. Conscious that the greatest danger would be to disturb the smooth running of the machine, they operate as carefully as they can, gingerly putting one foot in front of the other. They are not sleepwalking. They are walking the tightrope.

If we were simply asleep, the solution to our

predicament would be obvious. They say you should never wake a sleepwalker, but that advice does not apply if someone is stumbling towards disaster. Of course you wake them up! The risk of what might happen if you startle people who are sleepwalking is nothing compared to what might happen if they remain oblivious to their surroundings. A nasty shock may be just what is required. But a nasty shock is rarely a good idea for someone on a tightrope. Calm is what's needed: no sudden movements, no false steps. The tightrope walker takes one step at a time.

Sleepwalking and tightrope walking are both features of contemporary democracy. It is what gives our politics its peculiar double quality of attentiveness and carelessness.

In the run-up to the 2008 financial crash, elected politicians and central bankers appeared to be asleep at the wheel. Risks were allowed to build up in the system because no one was thinking hard enough about the wider picture. Too many of the leading players behaved like glassy-eyed gamblers, unable to see beyond the next bet. Not any more. Since the crash, the behaviour of those charged with running the system has been more like tightrope walkers. The programme of quantitative easing and cheap money on which they have embarked is very risky – no one knows what its long-term consequences might be. There are no historical precedents. But neither the bankers nor the politicians are blind to the risks. They know it is hazardous. That is why they are so sensitive to the dangers of a false step. They tread carefully, eyes ahead, afraid to look down.

The solution Varoufakis sought to the Greek crisis foundered on the tension between these states of mind. He wanted to wake Europe up to the looming threat. But the forces he faced – the EU, the ECB, the German government – were not asleep at the wheel. They were already wide awake, and they saw his noisy, plate-smashing politics as a danger to the finely balanced system they were trying to preserve.

Each side in this contest appeared to their antagonists to be behaving as though they were in a trance. To Varoufakis, the troika were the sleepwalkers, unable to see round the next corner, where calamity was waiting. To the troika, Varoufakis was the oblivious gambler, incapable of acknowledging what was truly at stake. Because this is politics, both parties were driven by contingencies they struggled to control. There was no real conspiracy on either side. Yet politicians who appear to be in a trance-like state provide the fuel for conspiracy theories. The creature is asleep but it moves purposefully. Someone must be pulling the strings.

These are the perils of audience democracy. The spectators have to fight with their own conflicting impulses to do too much or to do too little. When politicians appear to be asleep it is tempting to shout 'Boo!' and see what happens. But if the politicians are awake and frightened to look down, hearing the audience explode in noise will not produce the desired effect. Tightrope walkers are not galvanised into action by the sound of the crowd. They are trained to ignore it. Their trance-like state deepens as the spectators grow more irritable. They can appear frozen, nervous of going forward or back. What happens then? The spectators might shout louder. Or they might give up and walk away.

Tightrope walking can be a creative act. The 2008 documentary film *Man on Wire* reconstructs the story of Philippe Petit's high-wire walk between the twin towers of the World Trade Center in the late summer of 1974. Petit nicknamed his escapade *'le Coup'* – it was organised in secret and carried out with a small group of collaborators, who helped him break into the buildings overnight and rig up the equipment he needed. Petit walked from tower to tower more than 400 metres above the ground, covering the distance between them eight times. An astonished crowd gathered below and Petit later said he could hear their murmuring and cheers. Seen now, there is something haunting about what Petit did. Part of the poignancy derives from the fact that the twin towers are no longer there. Yet it also comes from the spontaneity of the act itself. Petit's coup was neither cautious nor careless. It was a piece of genuine self-expression.

Contemporary democracy is haunted by a sense of what it has lost. Some of the loss is the capacity for genuine self-expression. We do not walk the tightrope. It is done for us, by functionaries who are motivated by their anxious desire not to fall. The noise of the crowd is not an integral part of the performance. It is another hazard to be faced in the attempt to keep upright and moving forwards. No one reaches the other side and then turns to come back just for the hell of it. The purpose of the performance is simply to keep aloft.

Democratic politics still has its reckless side. We elect politicians who promise to shake things up because the show has come to mean little to us. It has turned into a sterile and artificial performance. Trump is no joyful high-wire artist. He is a sleepwalker and a gambler, unconcerned by watching others fall. To wish to put him on the wire is to believe one of two things. Either there is a safety net. Or the whole performance is a sham.

At the same time, we indulge ourselves with dystopias. They have their sedative power, too. It is impossible to read *The Road* without being profoundly moved. The story of an unnamed father and son strug- gling for meagre survival in a wasted society speaks to the fragility of life, the power of the human spirit and the horrors that may yet await us. Many readers reported being galvanised into action by their raw response to that harrowing book. Parents got up in the night to wake their children and tell them how much they loved them. Then they slept better. Imagining the worst has a strange comfort. But it has no political power. *The Road* does not galvanise us into political action. It is an oddly consoling parable for a society of sleepwalkers and tightrope walkers.

3

Technological takeover!

PEOPLE LAUGH WHEN Al Gore claims to have invented the internet. So they should. It wasn't Gore. It was Mahatma Gandhi.

Forster's 'The Machine Stops' was first published in the *Oxford and Cambridge Review* in November 1909. Gandhi, then a youngish lawyer and civil rights activist living in South Africa, appears to have read the story on his sea journey home from London that month (the *Review* would have been in the ship's library and everyone on board must have had time to kill, even Gandhi). He was clearly affected by it. Gandhi spent most of the voyage writing *Hind Swaraj*, his manifesto for Indian independence from British rule. Forster's eerie vision of our networked future helped to inform Gandhi's idea of where Western civilisation was heading, and why India needed to be free of it.

In *Hind Swaraj*, Gandhi provides an uncannily prophetic picture of the coming age of Amazon, Uber and HelloFresh. Inspired by Forster, he laments where technology is taking us:

> Men will not need the use of their hands and feet. They will press a button and they will have their

clothing by their side. They will press another and they will have their newspaper. A third, and a motorcar will be waiting for them. They will have a variety of delicately dished up food. Everything will be done by machinery.[48]

Gandhi saw our growing dependence on these artificial pleasures and comforts as a mark of civilisational failure. Yet, as he writes in *Hind Swaraj*, 'this is considered the height of civilisation'.

Gandhi places much of the blame for what's gone wrong on modern representative democracy. A political system that depended on elected officials to take decisions on our behalf would never be able to rescue us from this artificial existence. How could it? Representative democracy was wholly artificial. It had become in thrall to machines. It operated through the party machine, the bureaucratic machine, the money machine. Citizens were passive consumers of their own political destiny. We press a button and we expect government to respond. It is no surprise that we are disappointed. What we get instead are cheap promises and outright lies.

For Gandhi, the ideal was a return to something more like the face-to-face politics of the ancient world, where human interaction was unmediated by machinery. He believed this could happen in an independent India, if its democracy was organised around village communities and traditional Indian values of 'self-rule' ('*Swaraj*'). India gained independence in 1947 but Gandhi's version of democracy never took hold. Today, though Gandhi's iconic status as the father of the nation is secure, Indian democracy is as artificial as it is anywhere. The party machine, the bureaucratic machine and the money machine remain in charge. Gandhi's century-old vision of a society governed by the people pressing buttons for the sake of the people pressing buttons has come to pass in the place he hoped would rescue us from it. The machine won.

Gandhi's preferred way of doing politics is far too demanding for most twenty-first century citizens. He wanted to break our reliance on modern medicine, on lawyers, on mechanical transportation and on artificial communication. He thought individuals should travel only as far as their legs would take them and to communicate only as far as their voices could carry. We can't live like that. Yet we can instinctively recognise that Gandhi was right about what our politics has become. Modern democracy is highly mechanical and deeply artificial. It does not provide an alternative to the complex systems that it purports to regulate. It copies them, by becoming increasingly complex and artificial itself.

There is always a counterpart to the fear of what happens if the machine stops. Gandhi articulates it. What happens if the machine doesn't stop? Where do we end up then? Gandhi was an improbable prophet of the future of digital technology. Still, he was better at it than many technologists are.

What the historian David Edgerton calls 'the shock of the old' applies to digital technology as much as to any other kind of technology – change rarely happens as fast as we think.[49] It takes place in a landscape where most objects are still the familiar ones. A world that is about to herald the arrival of self-driving cars also contains more bicycles than ever before. We tend to overstate how quickly technological transformation will make itself clear to us. This is especially true of people with a vested interest in making it happen. They want it to happen now.

We remain some way off from the long-promised dawn of machines with minds of their own. Many researchers into AI see the realistic prospect of truly intelligent machines as being twenty years away. They have been saying that for at least the last fifty years. The AI horizon keeps shifting twenty years ahead. Just as democracy will end at some point, so too will intelligent machines arrive eventually, and perhaps even suddenly. But we are not there yet. We are moving forwards rapidly but we are not getting much closer to our most lurid dreams of the future. Computers can do things that were unimaginable twenty years ago, and which are far beyond the power of the human mind. But they can't think like we can.

Waiting for the AI revolution that never comes can be a giant displacement activity. While we are worrying about the dawn of intelligent machines, unintelligent machines are already doing much of the work. Computers may not have learned how to think for themselves. But we have learned how to let them think for us. A machine does not have to be intelligent to perform tasks that traditionally fall within the ambit of human intelligence. All it takes is for the humans to franchise the work out to the machine, having first told the machine what to do.

Unintelligent but super-efficient machines are already doing a lot of the work in contemporary democracies. Political parties rely on large automated databases to help run their campaigns. Governments increasingly utilise big data systems to manage and deliver health-care and other public services. These machines do not seek to conquer us. They don't seek anything for them-selves – they are not capable of that level of volition. They are not merely our servants, but our slaves. We put them to use. Yet as writers about politics have warned for more than two thousand years, slavery is bad for the slave-owners too. It makes them slavish to their own, easily satisfied desires. It leaves them at the mercy of their unthinking whims.

The danger of unintelligent machines is that, as they grow in power and usefulness, they lure intelligent human beings into relying on them for too much. Machine learning currently allows computers to mine vast amounts of data for insights that no human could match, picking up the rules of the game as they go along. These are not intelligent insights – they lack depth, nuance and emotional resonance. Yet it is machine learning that enables self-driving cars to travel the roads more safely and reliably than any human-driven automobile could. It is machine learning that tells Google what you are searching for before you have quite realised it yourself. Without knowing what they are doing, machines can navigate the world we have built more successfully than we can.

It is not hard to conjure up a dystopian version of this future. Being able to deploy unthinking but immensely powerful and sophisticated mechanical workhorses is a way to grow fat and lazy, in mind if not in body. The car drives us; the Fitbit monitors us; the polibot decides for us. Why not franchise out all the difficult decisions to machines that can crunch the data for us? We might do this consciously, for the sake of an easier life; or we might do it unconsciously, because our growing reliance on these machines leaves us incapable of knowing when to stop. We can all recognise the signs. We spend hours sending and responding to pointless emails not because our computers are telling us that we must, but simply because we lack the capacity to break the spell. The only thing that frees us is when an even more accessible and immediate technology comes along. Then we get addicted to that. Costless convenience is its own curse.

In the political version of the nightmare, our

dependence on this technology leaves us ripe for exploitation. It won't be killer robots that enslave us. All it takes is ruthless individuals capable of using the machines to their own advantage. In the land of the technologically dependent, the savvy political operator is king. This is the scare story that currently haunts Western democracy and I will come back to it later in this chapter. Its visible signs are fake news and the micro-targeting of voters with machine-generated messages designed to trigger their individual prejudices. The power of computers to press our buttons could spell the end of democracy if it falls into the wrong hands.

But this story doesn't have to be dystopian and this chapter is not simply about the worst that could happen. The machines are still just machines. Bad people can put them to bad purposes, but most people are decent human beings. Even if the vast majority of modern citizens cannot live Gandhi's ascetic version of the good life, that does not mean they have failed. For these people – for us – technology can help improve our experience of the world. Convenience and comfort are not things to be sniffed at. Nor is trying to make democracy work more efficiently.

In the end, hugely powerful but unthinking machines are not really our slaves because they do not suffer at the hands of us their masters. We are not corrupted by using them in the way that a human being is corrupted by using another human being as though that person were just an object. These machines are just objects. We can use them as we wish.

So why shouldn't we use them to improve our democracy rather than to destroy it? If our political institutions are struggling at present because they cannot find workable solutions to seemingly intractable problems, then machine learning looks like it should be a help rather than a curse. Machines that cannot be distracted by their emotional responses to the evidence might be just what we need. Democracies are far too easily distracted. People *feel* that things ought to be one way or the other, regardless of what they are told. Machines don't. They follow the evidence wherever it leads them.

The problem-solving capacity of new technology has already enhanced other professions. Some computers can already diagnose a patient's illness better than any individual doctor can – because the machine has access to a vastly greater body of relevant information. This does not have to put the doctor out of business. It might make her or him a better doctor. The machine solves the technical problem; the doctor humanises the solution, by talking intelligently and sympathetically to the patient about what it means, person to person. It will be a long time before computers can do sympathy as well (though some AI specialists will tell you it is only about twenty years away). The same could hold for politics. The machine solves the problem; the politician helps us to understand what the solution means. Democracy might get better.

For this to happen, though, some other things will have to happen first. Politics needs to regain a measure of control over these machines and over the people who currently control them. Otherwise there is a danger that, instead of using the machines to help solve our problems, we limit ourselves to the kind of problems that can be solved by machines. Technology by itself does not determine our future. But it will if we let it.

A DYSTOPIA IS ONLY A BAD DREAM, just as a utopia is a good one – these are places that don't actually exist. A world populated by immensely powerful, unthinking machines is not a dream. We already live in it. We have done for a long time. It is the modern world. The question of how to live with these machines has always been at the heart of modern politics.

Gandhi was far from alone in seeing Western democracy as dominated by the political machine. Max Weber, the great German sociologist who was Gandhi's contemporary, thought the same. The difference was that Weber recognised there was little we could do about it. He accepted that modern democracy was bound to be thoroughly mechanical. Political parties were 'machines' – soulless constructions designed to withstand the daily grind of winning and holding power. Bureaucracy was 'an iron cage'. Unlike Gandhi, Weber could imagine no way for our societies to function without these vast, soulless structures. It made democratic politics a peculiarly alienating business. What gave us a voice was also what made us cogs in the machine. That, for Weber, was the modern condition.

Jeremy Bentham, the philosopher and democratic reformer who was writing a century before Weber and Gandhi, was mocked by his critics as a 'calculating machine'. He seemed to have reduced politics to a search for the algorithm of human happiness. He wished to know which levers to pull. But Bentham was anything but heartless. He desperately wanted the politics of his time to work better: to be less cruel, less arbitrary and more tolerant of human difference. That meant democratising it. But it also meant making it more formulaic in order to free it from prejudice. Bentham accepted that to humanise politics you had to be willing to dehumanise it first.

Going even further back, the definitive image of modern politics is a picture of a robot. It comes from the middle of the seventeenth century:

In Thomas Hobbes's *Leviathan* (1651), the state is described as an 'automaton', brought to life through the principle of artificial motion.[50] This robotic state does not think for itself. It has no thoughts apart from the ones that are given it by its component human parts. But if the structure is right, a modern state can turn human inputs into rational outcomes by stripping them of their capacity to feed violent mistrust. Hobbes's robot is meant to be scary: scary enough that any individual would think twice before taking it on. But it is also meant to be reassuring. The modern world is full of all sorts of machines. This is the machine that was created to master them for our benefit.

Hobbes understood that the state needed to be built in the image of the things it was trying to control. It had to look human, since if it couldn't control human beings it would be useless. But it also had to be machine-like: a robot with a human face. This robot was needed to rescue us from our natural instincts. Left to their own devices, human beings were liable to tear any political community to shreds. For Hobbes that was one of the lessons of the ancient world: when politics is based on unmediated human interaction it ends up as a violent free-for-all. All ancient states fell apart eventually. Nothing so purely human is built to last. But a modern machine can be.

However, there were two big risks with turning the state into a giant automaton. The first was that it wouldn't be powerful enough. Other artificial creatures that were more ruthless, more efficient, more robotic – and, by implication, less human – might turn out to be stronger. The second was that it would too closely resemble the things it was designed to regulate. In a world of machines, the state might go native. It could become entirely artificial. This is the original fear of the modern age: not what happens when the machines become too much like us, but what happens if we become too much like machines.

The machines that most frightened Hobbes were corporations. We have grown so used to living with corporations that we have stopped noticing how strange and machine-like they are. For Hobbes, they were another species of robot. They exist for our convenience, but they can acquire a life of their own. A corporation is an unnatural assemblage of human beings, given artificial life in order to do their bidding. The danger was that the humans would end up doing the corporation's bidding instead.

Many of the things that we fret about when we imagine a future world of AIs are the same worries that have been harboured about corporations for centuries. Corporations are man-made monsters. They have no conscience because they have no soul. They are able to live longer than people do. Some of them almost appear to be immortal. Corporations, like robots, can emerge unscathed from the wreckage of human affairs. During the first half of the twentieth century, German society underwent a near-death experience. The scale of the human destruction was mind-blowing. Yet some German corporations came through it all as if it had never happened. Some of the biggest German companies created in the nineteenth century are still among the biggest today – Allianz, Daimler, Deutsche Bank, Siemens. It is as though the madness of human beings is nothing to do with them.

At the same time, corporations are dispensable. Some might live for ever, but most of them have a very short shelf life. Humans create them and wind them up in the blink of an eye. Because they have no souls and no feelings, it doesn't matter. Some corporations are nothing but shells. We proliferate them unthinkingly. They also proliferate themselves. Corporations spew out further corporations – shells within shells – simply to make it hard for ordinary human beings to understand what they are up to. One of the nightmare scenarios for our robot future is what would happen if the robots could self-replicate. We already have some idea of what that would be like – it's the corporate world.

Hobbes believed that the only way to control corporations was to empower the artificial state. He was right. Before the eighteenth century, states and corporations competed for territory and influence. And there was no guarantee that the state would come out on top. The East India Company outperformed and outmatched the state in many parts of the world. This corporation fought wars. It raised taxes. On the back of these activities, it became enormously powerful as well as very wealthy. But as the modern state has grown in power and authority, and particularly as it has democratised over the past two hundred years, it has asserted itself. The East India Company was nationalised by the British state in 1858. Roosevelt's trust-busting at the start of the twentieth century, when he broke up the monopoly power of America's largest corporations, was further testament to the new-found confidence of the democratic state. Yet it wasn't really Roosevelt who did it. It was Roosevelt as the human face of the vast American political machine. This was the Leviathan in action.

Weber was right: modern democracy can't escape the machine. What Gandhi sought in that regard was utopian. But the democratic machine can help to humanise the artificial modern world. This has long been a part of the promise of democratic politics. Until now, the promise has been largely kept.

A common complaint against twenty-first century democracy is that it has lost control of corporate power. Big companies hoard wealth and influence. They fuel inequality. They despoil the planet. They don't pay their taxes. For many corporations these kinds of complaints come with the territory – banks and oil companies have heard them all before. But banks and oil companies are no longer the world's most powerful corporations. That mantle has passed to the technology giants: Facebook, Google, Amazon and Apple. These companies are young and fresh-faced. They believe that what they are doing is good. They are not used to being loathed. The state is not sure how to deal with monsters like these.

Still, they are just corporations. If American democracy found the strength to face down corporate titans like Standard Oil at the start of the twentieth century, why shouldn't it take on Google and Facebook today? Mark Zuckerberg is mind-bogglingly wealthy. But John D. Rockefeller was on some measures the richest man who has ever lived. That wasn't enough to save his corporate creation. All corporations have an off switch. The state knows where to find it. Or at least it used to.

No corporation, however rich or powerful, can exist without the support of the state. Corporations are created in law and they operate through the web of rules and regulations that the state provides to manage them. The growing complexity of the rules makes taking on any big corporation a daunting task, and many corporations are adept at seeking out the jurisdiction that suits them best. The existence of rival sets of rules created by rival states – and by non-state organisations like the EU – makes the job of regulation and control even harder. But it is not impossible. It takes political will. The complex machinery of the modern state often obscures the presence of political will. We can't seem to find the ghost in the machine when we need it. None the less, it is in there somewhere.

In the past democracies have discovered the will to take on corporate power. Can they do it again? Perhaps. But these historical analogies may be a false comfort in the digital age. Today's corporate behemoths exist in a political culture that has grown very accommodating to their power. In the US this was cemented by the Supreme Court decision in the Citizens United case of 2010 to grant corporations the same rights to free speech as individual citizens. What this meant in practice was that their right to buy political influence became effectively unchecked. If we want our creature to outmatch their creature, we need to make sure we haven't sold it out to them first.

Google and Facebook are very different beasts from Standard Oil. Each has a far greater reach. They don't just monopolise one thing. They monopolise many things at once. They produce the stuff on which we have come to depend in our everyday lives – we rely on their platforms and products in order to communicate. At the same time, they influence what we say to each other, by shaping what we see and hear. Zuckerberg is both an industrialist and a media magnate: Rockefeller and William Hearst rolled into one. This Citizen Kane doesn't just own the digital printing presses. He owns the digital oil wells, too.

There is no guarantee that this power will last – corporations come and go. But for now, it looks truly formidable. When the *Economist* tried to devise a cover illustration to capture corporate power on such a scale, it reached much further back in time. The magazine portrayed Zuckerberg as a Roman emperor, deciding on our fate with a thumbs up or a thumbs down. He has been compared to an Egyptian pharaoh, with seemingly god-like powers. Were any of that really the case, there would be less for us to worry about. The divine authority of ancient rulers was ultimately exposed as an illusion. A pharaoh is no match for the machine-like efficiency of the modern state. All god-like emperors have feet of clay, even twenty-first century ones. The real threat comes if Facebook is able to mimic the Leviathan.

Look again at Hobbes's picture of the state. Suitably updated, it could be a picture of Facebook. Just put Zuckerberg's head at the top. He is no emperor. He is the sovereign of a vast corporate machine, whose component parts are made from the input of huge numbers of individual human beings. These people provide Facebook with its power, but they share very little of that power themselves. What they get in return is the freedom to do their own thing. That was the promise of Hobbes's state, too. Hobbes didn't offer the citizens control over the monster they had created. What he offered them instead was control over their own lives in exchange for giving life to an artificial creature that could underpin their shared existence. He traded them personal freedom for political control.

Over time, that bargain was to prove insufficient. Most people wanted more control. Specifically, what they wanted was more democracy: the ability to control their political overlords, or at least to replace them with ones they liked better given the chance. The modern state evolved to include more and more of its citizens in its decision-making, as opposed to simply including them in its embrace. The same might happen to Facebook. It could democratise over time. To use its services might in due course provide its members with the right to help decide on its policies, as happens in democratic states. History teaches us that the Leviathan can be tamed.

However, history never has just one lesson. To get from Hobbes's Leviathan to a fully developed form of modern democracy took about three hundred years. Three hundred years in the life of a corporation like Facebook is an eternity – even thirty years may be too long to wait. If Facebook is going to be tamed any time soon, it will need to be done by the power possessed by states, which are the machines we invented for that purpose. This can't simply be the people v. Facebook. It will have to be Leviathan v. Leviathan.

Which giant will win? It is not a level playing field. Hobbes's Leviathan holds the sword. Facebook doesn't. It cannot compel obedience through violence or the threat of violence. What Zuckerberg's creature has in its hand is the smartphone. Its power is connective, not coercive. It has to rule us through habit, persuasion and distraction. Modern citizens cannot choose to exit the state – it was part of the Hobbesian bargain that there would be no out. A consumer can choose to leave Facebook at any time. Facebook's power depends on making that choice increasingly empty. Zuckerberg needs his people to feel that they have nowhere else to go.

Network power, which is the basis of Zuckerberg's extraordinary reach, operates by drawing people in. Facebook keeps gathering new members because it has so many members already: the value of joining increases with each new person who joins. The more Facebook is able to interpose itself in the relationships that individuals already have, the more need other individuals will have of it if they wish to maintain their existing relationships. This is not the power of brute force. It is simply the weight of numbers. When an upstart network comes along that tempts people away, Facebook buys it (as it has done with Instagram, WhatsApp and others). The bigger Facebook is the bigger it gets because its vast purchasing power puts up huge barriers to entry for anyone else.

So Facebook has something to compensate for the absence of the sword. In that picture of the Leviathan (page 128), it is not just the giant looming over the landscape. It is also turning into the town in the foreground. It has started to become the place where people live.

If the contest were simply giant v. giant, the state would win. The state doesn't just have an army, a police force and a judicial system. It also retains control over the currency, which is the other great weapon in its arsenal. For Hobbes, the ability to determine what would count as money was one of the primary powers a state can possess. To abandon it would be to abdicate political control. That remains true. States will happily devolve monetary authority to central banks. They do this to keep the value of their money safe from outside interference. They do not give it up to corporate rivals.

Until Google and Facebook have their own currencies, both still have reason to be afraid of the US Federal Reserve. They need the state to provide them with a store of value. Without it, their own value is uncertain. That is why Bitcoin and other digital currencies are so attractive to many technologists – they open up the possibility of liberating them from their dependence on the state. Google and Facebook may well have their own money one day, or at least their own money-like equivalent that can serve as a store of value, unit of account and medium of exchange – it is a far more realistic prospect than either ever acquiring its own army. But it is probably at least twenty years away.

It is power over the sword and power over money that has enabled the state to defeat overmighty corporations in the past. But if this new contest is network v. network, then the big tech companies have other advantages. Facebook can claim nearly two billion members, bigger than any state or any empire. It can infiltrate itself into people's lives in a way that no state can. By providing the space in which they share their experiences, it has the capacity to shape how they live. States do that by making rules which they can back up with force if necessary. Social networks do it by influencing what people see and what they hear.

It is still possible to imagine the US state deciding to terminate Facebook if it really wanted to and if it could find the political will. It has that power. Facebook is a corporation and corporations have an off switch. But Facebook is also a vast social network. You can turn off the machine. You can't so easily unplug the place where people live.

Yet the shock of the old applies to politics as well. Even as the world has been transformed by these new forms of corporate power, familiar patterns of human behaviour persist. When Trump won the presidency, he summoned the heads of the dominant Silicon Valley firms to meet him at Trump Tower. Most of them showed up as asked. Zuckerberg couldn't make it, but Sheryl Sandberg, Facebook's COO, was there. So were leaders from Google, Apple and Amazon. Some companies were deliberately snubbed. Jack Dorsey, the head of Twitter, was not invited. Twitter may be Trump's megaphone, but he is not going to be beholden to anyone.

Trump wanted to establish the traditional hierarchy. Silicon Valley might look like it has a kind of power and reach that Washington can only dream of, but no mere corporate chief gets to tell the president what to do. Gathered round Trump's table, with the president in the centre, they had to listen to him. The pecking order was clear.

Then the tech titans dispersed. Next to nothing came of this meeting. Like so much of Trump's presidency, it was just for show. He had proved his point – he calls, they come over. But his point was a largely empty one.

Trump thinks hierarchically – he wants to make sure that people get told. That is only one part of politics, which is why Trump comes across as such a one-dimensional politician. Vertical relationships have to be supplemented with horizontal ones, through which people work together to get things done. Trump's failure to supplement his vertical relationships is a big reason why he has found it so hard to get things done.

The most successful democratic politicians do it far better: they draw people in. The hierarchy gets supplemented by the network. The Leviathan has fearsome weapons at its disposal. But the democratic state derives its true strength from the combination of top-down authority and broad inclusivity. The sword only works when the people who live under it believe in the right of the government to exercise it on their behalf.

Like a modern state, Facebook is both a hierarchy and a network. If anything, it is far more hierarchical than any democratic state: Zuckerberg and his immediate circle exercise an extraordinary level of personal control. It is more like a medieval court than a modern polity. Power flows from the top. At the same time, its network is far broader and more inclusive than any state could achieve. Facebook has many more people on its books than any democracy. They do more with it and through it than they do with and through any political instrument. The state provides us with services. Facebook helps us curate our lives. The state can make us feel secure. Facebook can make us feel loved.

The great political weakness of Facebook is that its hierarchy and its network are so disconnected. The top-down organizational structure of the corporation and the massively dispersed scope of its social network are entirely at odds with each other. Zuckerberg is a prince. His people might as well be serfs. He likes to talk the language of 'community' in an attempt to hold the whole enterprise together. 'Progress now requires humanity coming together not just as cities or nations, but also as a global community' is how he put it in the personal mission statement he released in February 2017.[51] He sounds like a twenty-first century businessman but he also sounds like a pope, so little do his pronouncements feel constrained by the need to answer to anyone for his views.

Can Zuckerberg tell the president of the United States what to do? No. Can Facebook's two billion users outvote the two hundred million-strong electorate of the United States? No. But could Facebook undermine the way that American democracy operates? Yes. The challenge comes not first-hand but at one remove. The sword still beats the smartphone. Facebook will not take down the Leviathan in mortal combat. But it could weaken the forces that keep modern democracy intact. Even if it can't bring its own hierarchy and network together, it could still pull the hierarchy and the network of the democratic state apart.

DAVE EGGERS'S 2013 NOVEL *The Circle* describes a giant tech company of the near future.[52] This fictional corporation is called 'The Circle'. It could be Google or it could be Facebook – it reads like an amalgam of the two. It is a business of extraordinary global reach that seeks to connect human beings across the full range of their activities. It does this by encouraging them to rate everything they do on its platforms, thereby making itself the primary measure of value in their lives. At the same time, the organisation is secretive and mysterious in its internal operations. It is run by its founders, the three 'Wise Men', who pose as gurus and wield extensive, arbitrary power. The world rates itself on their network. The Wise Men decide the uses to which their network can be put.

The Circle is often described as dystopian but really it is a satire. It brings out the absurd mismatch between the claims to universal community made by companies like Facebook and their cult-like exclusivity. These corporations employ relatively few people. To work there is to belong to a super-elite that is barely integrated into the lives of the communities they are in the business of building. Google drives its employees to work in customised buses that connect the parts of San Francisco where no one else can afford to live to the parts of Silicon Valley where no one else is qualified to work.

In the summer of 2017, to correct for the perception that he is somehow aloof from the everyday world, Zuckerberg embarked on a listening tour of the United States. His goal was to learn more about how ordinary people live. 'My work is about connecting the world and giving everyone a voice,' he wrote on Facebook in January. 'I want to personally hear more of those voices this year.'[53] His arrival in various outposts of small-town America had to be prepared by a praetorian guard of publicists and security operatives, who cleared restaurants, vetted families and sourced suitable locations. This enabled Zuckerberg to write gushingly about North Dakota, as one journalist put it, 'as though he were Christopher Columbus himself and had just discovered that the place existed'.[54] The glorified road trip fuelled speculation that he is planning to run for president one day.

Facebook's mission statement is: 'Give people the power to build communities and bring the world closer together.' In Eggers's novel, the mantra of his imagined digital leviathan is: 'Close the Circle.' The goal is full interconnectivity. If everyone were truly linked to everyone else there would be no room for anyone to feel neglected. One of the founders of the Circle applies this principle to democracy. 'As we know here at the Circle,' he tells a company meeting, 'with full participation comes full knowledge. We know what Circlers want because we ask ... We can get very close, I think, to 100% participation. One hundred percent democracy.'[55] The way to do it would be to ensure that everyone has a Circle account on which they depend for their everyday transactions and then to shut that account to anyone who won't participate in democratic decision-making. Either you tell us what you want or we won't let you want anything. As a result, participation becomes universal. And democracy becomes corporate tyranny.

A corporation like Facebook can never 'do' democracy better than a state. The gap between the inclusivity of its rhetoric and the exclusivity of its practices is a yawning chasm. What Eggers brings out is not the direct threat but the risk of collateral damage. The idea of closing the circle is ridiculous. But at a time of growing frustration with representative democracy it is also seductive. Modern democracy is riddled with holes. Many people do feel neglected. Their views seem to count for little and their representatives often appear uninterested in hearing them out. Contemporary populism feeds off this sense of disconnect. Even if social media can't provide a substitute for modern democracy, it can offer tempting ways to plug some of the gaps.

One of the deepest contemporary irritations with representative democracy is how slow and clumsy it can be, particularly when compared to the immediate satisfactions available online. The modern state remains a large and cumbersome machine. Online communities move much quicker. Democracy, with its checks and balances, its bureaucracy and its procedures, often seems too unwieldy for the twenty-first century.

In *The Circle*, Eggers imagines how these frustrations might play out in the realm of law enforcement. Dangerous criminals sometimes abscond and the bureaucratic state is too slow to catch up with them. Why not publish their details online and see how quickly a social network of concerned citizens can find them? In Eggers's version, a child killer is hunted down and lynched in the space of twenty minutes, with twenty million people watching and participating online. An anonymous face is shown on the screen, the crowd rapidly sources her true identity and ferrets out her hiding place, and camera-wielding citizens turn up at her place of work to confront her with their righteous fury. For the executives of the Circle, this is another example of pure democracy in action.

Pure democracy is a terrifying thing. It's all too easy for the crowd to turn on any individual who displeases it. In ancient Athens, public figures who lost favour could be ostracised or murdered by the demos. Alexis de Tocqueville, writing about American democracy in 1835, traced the American taste for lynching to the country's democratic origins. Tocqueville called it 'the tyranny of the majority': given the chance, the many feel empowered to take out their angry frustrations on the vulnerable few. The long history of modern representative democracy has been a largely successful attempt to tame these wilder impulses. We don't lynch any more. We don't tar and feather. We don't ostracise. Except on Twitter.

Online witch hunts are not the real thing. The lynching is virtual. But the violence is real: to be on the receiving end of the online mob is to suffer an assault from which it can be very hard to recover. The victims of these attacks suffer physical harm. Depression and sickness are commonplace. Suicide can follow. Twitter is sometimes described as being like the Wild West. But really it is the closest thing we have to the democracy of the ancient world: fickle, violent, empowering. People have rediscovered the liberating effects of being able to gang up on individuals who have displeased them. It is exhilarating. And it can be deadly.

Far from being unmediated by machinery, online mob violence is conducted entirely through the machine. It has an inhuman quality. Ancient democracy was redeemed by being face-to-face: the demos had to look its victims in the eye. When it didn't – when it was asked to pass judgement on generals who were languishing overseas – it found it much easier to condemn. The

Twitter version of direct democracy is more dangerous because it is unlimited by the constraints of physical space and personal knowledge.

In one of the most notorious examples of an online witch hunt, Justine Sacco, a corporate PR executive, lost her job, her friends and her social standing after she published a joke on Twitter about race and AIDS before boarding a flight to South Africa. ('Going to Africa. Hope I don't get AIDS. Just kidding. I'm white!' is the full text of what she wrote.)[56] The world took immediate offence. By the time she landed, she found herself on the receiving end of an unstoppable torrent of abuse and death threats. Hers was the same journey from London to Cape Town that Gandhi had taken a century earlier. Being free from distraction for a few weeks at sea gave Gandhi the time to gather his thoughts. Maybe Sacco was hoping for a little of the same during her brief time in the air. Many of us do. What she found was that ten hours of isolation were enough to destroy her life.

To call this democracy in action might sound absurd. But that is precisely the threat it poses: it makes a mockery of democracy. Twitter is not a viable way of doing politics. At best it offers a feeble imitation of democracy, in which the people get to vent their frustrations without having to face up to the consequences. The president of the United States gets to do the same, whenever he feels like it. This raw demagoguery shares some features with the direct democracy of the past, without its redeeming qualities. The mob is fearless when roused and shows no favour. Ordinary citizens can be its victims. So can prominent politicians. The knowledge that an inopportune remark or a careless gesture might undo a life's work has a chilling effect on everyone. Except, perhaps, for the president of the United States.

How should politicians respond? Eggers suggests one way they might, which is appeasement. Digital technology offers the possibility of pre-empting the frustrations of the mob by making sure that nothing is hidden from it. In *The Circle*, one particularly craven politician offers to wear a digital camera round his neck at all times, linked to an online account, so that everyone can see what is going on in every encounter he has. Other politicians, rightly, suspect that this is lunacy. If nothing is hidden, nothing of substance can be said, because everything will become a hostage to fortune. The chilling effect will be complete. But when reasonable politicians try to make this case in public, the crowd turns on them. Why won't they reveal what they are up to? What are they trying to hide? In the land of the totally transparent, the partially private person is a crook. Within weeks, all politicians find themselves being fixed up with round-the-clock honesty cameras.

Representative democracy longs for what it can't have. We are permanently tempted by the possibility of closing the gaps that exist in our politics: to make it more honest, more responsive, more complete. Digital technology vastly enhances those temptations. Why not hold politicians more directly to account for everything they do? Why let them get away with hiding the truth from the people whose interests they are supposed to represent? Why not expose them?

We all want trustworthy politicians. Knowing what politicians are up to at all times might look like a way for us to trust them completely. But that is not trust. It is oversight, which is the opposite of trust. Once we know everything that is going on, trust becomes meaningless. We have no need to trust people who can never betray us: they might as well be machines. The precondition for trust is the possibility that we will be disappointed. To rule out disappointment is to give up on trusting anyone. It is self-defeating.

It is also an illusion. We can never know every-thing. Politicians will always find somewhere to hide. The more openness we demand, the more secretive they will have to be in order to keep some things hidden. The insistence on absolute transparency simply places a greater premium on finding secure hiding places. When we ferret those out, our fury will be fearsome.

Representative democracy cannot close the circle. It depends on the spaces that exist between the people and their politicians; between the taking of a decision and its evaluation by the public; between the act of will and the act of judgement. It depends on there being enough time to reflect on what we have done. It presupposes disap-pointment. It is a deeply frustrating business. But it is the frustration – the rubbing along without ever coming together – that ensures that the relationship between the network and the hierarchy holds. Facebook doesn't do frustration.

All representative democracy can do is to try to square the circle. It is impossible. That's the point.

Another of the persistent frustrations with contem-porary democracy, along with its unresponsiveness, is its inherent artificiality. Nothing seems more artificial than political parties. As Gandhi pointed out, political parties exist to stop people thinking for themselves. The party tries to tell the politician which line to take. The party tries to tell the voter which politician to vote for. Parties get in the way of a direct encounter between the people and their representatives. They are tools for winning power. They are arcane and bureaucratic. It's their job to make politics as mechanical as possible.

Nevertheless, when they do their job well they conceal their artificiality behind a human face. Charismatic political leaders can persuade the voters that the party is more than just a vote-grabbing machine. It stands for something: justice, security, freedom. Meanwhile, the membership of a political party can imbue the mechanism with a life of its own. The most successful political parties of modern times have managed to provide their members with a genuine sense of belonging.

Those days seem over. Many mass membership political parties are in precipitous decline. The British Conservative Party, which had more than three million people on its books in the 1950s, has barely 100,000 left. Their average age is over 65. Plenty of its previous members had scant interest in politics. They saw the party as a social club, somewhere to go to dance, gossip and with a bit of luck meet a future wife or husband. Today, to belong to the party is to signal a very particular interest in politics, given how few people share it. Only the most eccentric would use it as a dating agency. It adds to the air of artificiality. Without members, political parties look more and more like shells of what they once were.

Meanwhile, party politics is growing more partisan. What were once loose coalitions have become strident and intolerant mouthpieces for particular points of view. This is most noticeable in the US, where the two-party system was traditionally the most capacious: Republicans and Democrats were once broad churches with both liberal and conservative wings and significant areas of overlap. Now the parties have sorted the electorate into sharply divided camps. A core of politically committed members pulls the parties apart; at the same time, ordinary voters are becoming less and less likely to encounter people from the other side. Republicans and Democrats don't live in the same districts – at least, not the carefully gerrymandered districts constructed for them by party politicians – they don't socialise together and they don't watch the same news. In 1980 only 5 per cent of Republicans said they wouldn't want their kids to marry a Democrat. By 2010 that figure had risen to 49 per cent.[57]

Charisma at the top of mainstream political parties also appears increasingly rare. Weber thought that part of the point of the party machine was to winnow out the true politicians from the functionaries. A genuine political leader would rise above the grind of daily politics to offer a sense of vision. Everyone else would fade into the background. Now the functionaries and the leaders are harder than ever to tell apart. Most professional politicians have never worked at anything else. They rise through the machine, not above it.

This is a story of long-term decline. But, like so much else, the social media revolution has accelerated it. Online communities offer a plethora of different ways to discover a sense of belonging. We don't need politics to be our social club when there are so many other kinds on offer. The grind of conventional party politics – sitting in long meetings on uncomfortable chairs in drafty rooms, tramping the streets, organising campaigns – can seem like a pale imitation of the gratification to be found on social networks. Of course, it is now possible to do some of these things online, too: the meetings can be virtual; the door-knocking can take place via smartphones. But that just highlights how much else is available at the click of a button.

As the appeal of old-fashioned party politics declines, the people who still choose to take part in it appear to be increasingly at odds with everyone else. It has turned into a cliquish activity. Part of what motivates the online abuse that gets directed at party politicians is the feeling that they are their own little club. Why else would they persist with it, except to look out for each other and for the donors who bankroll them? We hanker for politicians who don't behave like politicians. We want them to be real people, whereas so many of them come across as automatons. In the digital machine age, the mechanical quality of party politics has become its curse.

The result has been that many established political parties have taken an unprecedented battering at election time. In the French presidential election of 2017, neither of the two main parties of left and right that have dominated French politics for more than fifty years made it to the second round of voting. The electorate treated them as though they were relics of the past. The socialists were reduced to near oblivion. Their candidate, Benoît Hamon, polled barely 6 per cent of the vote. In the legislative elections that followed, the party lost nearly nine-tenths of its representatives in parliament. Mainstream parties have been wiped out in the Netherlands, in Greece and in Italy. Conventional parties of left and right look vulnerable to a similar fate almost everywhere in the democratic world.

By contrast, the political parties that have proved most successful in recent years are the ones that have turned themselves into social movements. Macron won the 2017 French presidency at the head of En Marche, a movement he had established only a year earlier. He was at pains to insist it was not a conventional political party. It was designed to be spontaneous, fresh and made up of real people, not politicians. In Britain, the Labour Party has bucked the trend of other declining social democratic parties in Europe by recasting itself as a social movement. Offering those who join a voice that can be used against the party's representatives in parliament, it has revived its mass membership. Its present leader, Jeremy Corbyn, repeatedly insists that the members are not there to be used by the MPs but the other way round.

In the United States, Trump won the presidency by running his own political movement against the Republican Party elite. Sanders almost did the same by running against the Democratic Party establishment. In India, Modi heads a personal movement as much as he does a political party. So does Erdogan in Turkey. Populists are at the forefront of movement politics. But this trend goes beyond populism. Macron, the supposed saviour of Europe from the populist scourge, used movement politics to defeat Marine Le Pen, the candidate of the far-right National Front. Le Pen found herself outflanked. Over time, her movement had turned into something more like a political party.

These successful movements benefit from the power of network effects. People join because other people join: they want to be where the action is. Political movements use social media and online communication to draw voters in. They grow quickly and offer more immediate and direct political involvement than can be had from conventional party politics. For now, they look like the only forms of representative democracy that can cope with the demands of the digital age.

However, coping is not the same as managing. Social movements are at risk of turning into the things they are trying to exploit. En Marche hasn't simply taken advantage of Facebook. It has come to resemble it. Its network is broad. But its hierarchy is steep. The man at the top stands aloof. Macron has been derided for comparing himself to the Roman god Jupiter. Early in his presidency he invited his deputies to Versailles, where he addressed them as though he were a cross between de Gaulle and Louis XIV. Yet the person he really resembles is Zuckerberg. He talks the language of community while hoarding his personal authority. In the absence of a conventional party structure, he struggles to find a means of bridging the two.

The British Labour Party under Corbyn has become similarly adept at making use of Facebook and other social networks to spread its message. Much of this happens without direct party involvement: partisan news sites go out of their way to blur the lines between reporting, clickbait and advocacy. At the same time, the party is an uneasy mix of direct democracy and personality cult. The members are meant to call the shots. But the leader can do no wrong. And woe betide anyone who stands between them.

The intolerance of many contemporary political movements – their vicious disdain for dissent – is often blamed on the groupthink that proliferates online. But it has as much to do with the basic structural problem that any movement has to face in the digital age. Having supplanted the political party as the organising instrument of modern politics, it has nothing left to break up its own echo chambers. That was the party's job.

The political scientist and historian Mark Lilla has recently described political parties as 'machines for reaching consensus through compromise'.[58] Like many others, Lilla blames identity politics for the mess that parties now find themselves in. The purity of the political experience increasingly counts for more than the outcome of the political process. But it is also true that we have grown increasingly tired of the fakery of machine politics, when more authentic-seeming collective experiences are available online. We want the real deal, forgetting that all the available versions are mediated by machinery.

Unlike political movements, political parties were never intended to *be* democracy. They were the glue that held representative democracy together. It is not clear that democracy can work without them. All we are left with are the bits: networks, leaders, crowds, elections, identities, mobs. Try building something out of that.

Social networks have made representative democracy seem fake. The fake versions that exist online appear more real. For now, we have destroyed something without knowing how to replace it. The only replacement is a hollow version of the thing we had before. The machine lost. The machine won.

WHAT HAPPENED TO THE democratic promise of the internet revolution? Digital technology once looked like it might change the rules of the game. Even if it couldn't close the circle of democracy, it could at least provide us with new ways of holding politicians to account. The modern state had always monitored its citizens. Now, finally, a technology appeared that seemed to offer citizens a chance to monitor it back. This did not have to be total transparency. It could simply be a way of turning the tables. Democracy should have been the beneficiary.

Part of Hobbes's inspiration for the idea of the Leviathan came from the creature of Greek mythology known as Argus Panoptes – the many-eyed monster that never sleeps. Hobbes wanted his state to have eyes in the back of its head. Otherwise there could be no true security, since political trouble can break out in the most unexpected places. Bentham created a different version of the same idea. He designed a prison he called the Panopticon. It was constructed on a circular model that would allow the governor to keep permanent watch on the inmates.

Whistleblower Edward Snowden's nickname for the

National Security Agency (NSA), whose secret mass surveillance operations he revealed to the world, was 'the Panopticon'. Bentham's original purpose in designing his prison was to ensure that convicted criminals did not use prison as an opportunity to conspire with each other. The governor couldn't hear everything that went on, so Bentham wanted to ensure he could always see who was mixing with whom. The NSA has defended its surveillance programme on the grounds that it is merely looking at the metadata of personal communications. It does not listen in on private conversations. It simply records who is in contact with whom. Snowden's nickname is entirely appropriate.

Representative democracy has always been a watching game. We watch them, to make sure they don't take advantage of the power we have given them. They watch us, to make sure we don't take advantage of the freedom they have given us. For most of the history of modern democracy, the politicians have had the upper hand in this relationship. They could call on the elaborate machinery of the state to do their surveillance work. We were left to our own devices. They could deploy new technologies to keep one step ahead. We got telephones; they got phone-tapping. We got television; they got CCTV. We were on the outside looking in; they were on the inside looking out. Then came the digital revolution.

With the dawn of the internet age the advantages promised to shift decisively towards the citizens. Networked technology put information beyond anyone's power to control. It became free and it was limitless. The Leviathan found itself exposed. We could pick away at it, discovering its secrets. Meanwhile, individual citizens could hide their own secrets in the vast expanse of cyberspace.

By the end of the twentieth century, in the first flush of euphoria that accompanies any revolution, the internet appeared to herald the next step in the triumph of democracy. Autocracies would fall. Political chicanery would be exposed. Information would flow from the places where it was being hoarded to the places where it was needed. The people would discover the truth about their politicians. They kept more secrets that we do, so they had more to lose.

We would finally gain the upper hand in the watching game.

We were wrong. Our mistake was to forget that they are better incentivised to keep their secrets than we are. It doesn't matter how much new information is available if we lack the desire to seek it out. We have the motive to discover more: knowledge is power. But we lack the motivation because acquiring knowledge remains hard work. Avoiding hard work is part of the point of representative democracy.

The other precious resource we lack is time. The political scientist Herbert Simon noted more than a generation ago that when information is plentiful, attention becomes the scarce resource. As a result, the Leviathan still has the edge. It is designed not to get distracted. We are.

The internet provides everyone with fresh opportunities to hoover up knowledge that would once have been kept hidden. The state remains much better equipped than any private citizen to take advantage. It can employ its own servants to do the work full-time. Only the most unusual individuals will devote all their private energies to checking up on the doings of the state. We tend to regard such people as deeply odd. We sometimes label them conspiracy theorists. Yet the most persistent conspiracy theorists work in government and spy on us.

Democratic states like the US and Britain have turned out to be prolific accumulators and hoarders of metadata. The democratic process in these countries has sought to put these activities under judicial oversight, but that is no solution to the difficulty of misaligned incentives. It simply replicates the problem. We are not watching them watching us. We are left hoping that our unelected public servants will watch them for us, even though they often appear barely qualified for the task. Who watches the watchers is the question to which representative democracy has no good answer once watching becomes too much like hard work.

The question of online surveillance has yet to acquire any clout as an electoral issue. Rand Paul, the Republican presidential candidate who did most to try to raise the subject in 2016, was swatted aside by Donald Trump with the ease of a man brushing off a fly. 'These are people who want to kill us,' Trump told a raucous crowd at an early candidates' debate in response to Paul, 'and you are objecting to us wanting to infiltrate their conversations? I don't think so! I don't think so!'[59]

So long as the watching game can be reduced to looking for terrorists, it is hard to object. As the saying goes, if you've got nothing to hide, you've got nothing to fear. The logic of politics has changed little since the Leviathan was invented. Contrary to earlier expectations, the internet has reinforced that logic rather than undermined it.

Digital technology has also reinforced rather than undermined the hold on power of many non-democratic regimes. Authoritarians can use it very effectively. Far from being a decisive weapon in the hands of freedom fighters, it has become an essential tool for keeping tracks on them. Many opposition groups in countries such as Ethiopia and Venezuela have found that their activities are much more easily infiltrated by authoritarian governments than authoritarian governments are infiltrated by them. Again, it is a question of incentives, time and human resources. Even corrupt and inefficient states tend to have more of each of these than their opponents, who are limited by their need to improvise. To this point the internet has not proved to be an autocracy-busting machine. It has turned into another useful tool of power.

What has changed is our basic understanding of when we are being watched. We have started to confuse them watching us for us watching them. This is not the world of Big Brother: the big lie that turns the television you stare at into a machine staring at you. In that case, the deception is so brazen that it is barely a deception at all. The Orwellian nightmare is to be under the kind of scrutiny that makes concealment futile because there is nowhere to hide. Internet surveillance makes concealment redundant because it is so hard to distinguish from the pursuit of genuine knowledge. We give ourselves away not by our passivity but by our curiosity.

Whenever we go online to dig up new information for ourselves, we end up handing over more information about ourselves, to all sorts of interested parties. Primarily, this happens to us as consumers. Our search history gives suppliers the information they need to target their products at us. When we look for the cheapest airline ticket, what we are really doing is enabling airlines to fix the price we might be willing to pay on the basis of our past behaviour. To search is to be searched. To seek a competitive advantage as an individual consumer is to give yourself away.

There is a political equivalent. The volume of information available online makes it much easier for voters to source their own news. It is easy to imagine that this is democracy in action – be vigilant! But what if our taste for certain kinds of news tells others what it is we prefer, and by looking for it we simply reveal our prejudices. Our desire to keep ourselves informed becomes the means for keeping tracks on us. It makes it possible to tailor the news to ensure we never actually discover anything new.

Fears about the spread of 'fake news' reflect this growing anxiety – how can we tell when our search for information will morph into an opportunity for further manipulation? A sophisticated political news operation could ensure that elections become a version of price-fixing: we only get to see what they already know we are willing to buy. The election of Trump and the Brexit vote in the UK were both accompanied by scare stories of this kind. A mysterious firm called Cambridge Analytica, funded by some prominent Trump supporters, appeared to be in the business of supplying information about individual voters based on their online identities. News feeds could be targeted accordingly. It is hard to know if it made any difference. But the margin of Trump's victory was sufficiently narrow – tens of thousands of voters in a few key states – to suggest that it just might have.

Meanwhile, the Kremlin has rediscovered its appetite for bombarding Western electorates with disinformation, based on extensive data harvesting. Bots on Twitter that pretend to engage in democratic debate are being programmed to make debate impossible, by turning all political argument into a never-ending shouting match. Bots that are very bad at impersonating human intelligence can still be very good at impersonating angry voters. All they have to do is make a lot of noise.

Unquestionably there are serious risks to democracy here. But for now they may be overblown. The micromanipulation of the electorate is almost certainly more difficult than it looks – a lot of what Cambridge Analytica is selling is simply hot air. We have a tendency to overstate the ease with which bad people can perform fiendishly complicated tasks. Fixing an election has always been hard work. Nerds tend to worry about James Bond villains taking over the world. But very few James Bond villains are actually nerds.

Many examples of fake news have little to do with a plot against democracy. They are nothing more than opportunism, something the internet supplies in abundance. A number of the most widely shared fraudulent news stories on Facebook during the 2016 presidential election were traced to the work of a few teenage hackers operating out of Macedonia ('Pope endorses Trump!' was one of the most popular). They were not in the pay of the Kremlin. They had simply discovered a way to make a quick buck, by driving online traffic past the political car crashes they had created.

The opportunity to make money from fake news arises out of the business model of the internet, which is advertising. The watching game has turned into a competition for our attention. It doesn't matter what holds our attention so long as it keeps us where advertisers can reach us. Pretend news will do the trick. So will real news, if it is interesting enough. Donald Trump was great for the *New York Times* and CNN as well as for the Macedonian hackers because he kept people reading and watching. If this were just about manipulation it would be easier to detect. But because it is about attention-seeking the line between active engagement and passive reception gets blurred.

Putin may be an evil genius, but it seems more likely that he is just another opportunist. So is Trump. Facebook – starting with Zuckerberg – has expressed genuine surprise at discovering how its technology can be used to spread fake news. The architects of the system are stumbling across its pitfalls along with the rest of us. There is every reason to believe Zuckerberg when he says that he wants to make the manipulation stop. He didn't intend for it to happen. That's the problem: no one did. It is just a side effect of being in the advertising business.

The visual imagery of spectators and performers that dominates modern conceptions of democracy is too humanistic for the digital age. These data-harvesting systems are just machines and machines don't observe the world like human beings do – they simply hoover up information. We mean little to them as individuals because they don't really see us as individuals – we are simply the unit that happens to be in front of the screen. People watch people. Machines process them. The threat to democracy is not manipulation. It is mindlessness.

Still, does it really matter if representative democracy gets reduced to a form of advertising? Many writers have long suspected that's all it has ever been. The economist Joseph Schumpeter, writing in 1942, defined democracy as a competition between teams of salesmen to get the voters to buy their product.[60] It's like buying soap powder. When we tire of one brand we can replace it with another.

In 1969 Joe McGinnis published *The Selling of the President 1968*, in which he described how Richard Nixon had been repackaged by Madison Avenue to make him more palatable to the American electorate.[61] Some readers at the time professed to be shocked at this manipulation of the democratic process; few would be shocked today. In the second half of the twentieth century the idea of democracy as a theatrical performance got supplanted by the idea of democracy as advertising.

First radio and then television changed the terms of the metaphor. The underlying idea did not alter much. They produce the politics; we consume it.

Elections are the final test of which product will sell, and fortunes have been made and lost providing politicians with a service to help them negotiate that marketplace. Are firms like Cambridge Analytica doing anything different? In one sense, no: this is just the latest version of the never-ending contest to see who is better at putting lipstick on the pig. But in another sense, something has fundamentally changed. Twentieth-century political salesmanship followed a distinctive rhythm. The goal was to close the deal at election time. They would come knocking on our doors and sometimes we would let them in. More often we would send them away. We did not invite them to set up shop in our homes.

Twenty-first century advertising has another set of imperatives. Closing the deal is less important than keeping the door permanently ajar. The competition for our attention means that the basic goal is to get us hooked on the medium. Online advertising is relentless. It follows us around. It aims to keep us on permanent alert.

Trump is the model politician for this version of democracy. For all his talk about the importance of sealing the deal, that has never been his primary mode of doing business. He is an attention seeker. Politicians are meant to behave differently once they have made the sale. Trump carried on after his victory as though he were still in campaign mode. He dominates the attention of the entire world, even as he fails to get anything done. As the neuroscientist Robert Burton put it in the *New York Times*, only half in jest: 'Donald Trump represents a black-box, first generation artificial-intelligence president, driven solely by self-selected data and wildly fluctuating ideas of success.'[62] He is the kind of bot you might get before general purpose intelligence kicks in.

Twenty-first century advertising preys on our cognitive biases, working with them to make sure we stay in the moment. Human beings have an inbuilt tendency to value immediate gratification over future benefits; to want to hold on to what they have; to seek reinforcement of their beliefs; to overestimate how much other people are paying attention to them; to underestimate how different their future selves might be from their present ones. Social networks are set up to satisfy these impulses, and so are the machines through which we access them. They are designed to be addictive. We keep checking our phones to find out what's new, so long as what's new chimes with what we would like to be true.

Representative democracy was intended to work against our cognitive biases, dimly though these might have been understood at the time. It puts barriers in the way of immediate gratification and slows down decision-making. It leaves room for buyer's remorse. The founders of the American republic did whatever they could to ensure that the political impulses of the people would get filtered through institutions designed to correct for their biases. That's what makes representative democracy so frustrating. It is rarely gratifying. It is not meant to be.

Buyer's remorse is relatively uncommon in the world of online commerce because there isn't the time for it. The act of purchase is simply followed by another purchase, targeted at us on the basis of what we have just bought. We keep buying the same things even as we try to correct for their defects, because we can't escape the messages that track our existing preferences. Democratic politics on this model is self-defeating rather than self-correcting. The tiger ends up chasing its tail. As a picture of democratic failure it has no historical parallel. The volume of democratic choice goes up. So does the futility.

Direct democracy, of the kind practised in the ancient world, was also designed to correct for our biases. Might this be a solution to the problem of our shared distraction? Philosophers from Aristotle onwards have argued that the best way to avoid individual errors of judgement is to pool our opinions so that the weight of numbers can tell. Collective decision-making works better than any individual's choices if our biases are allowed to cancel each other out. This is the wisdom of crowds.

The internet age has seen an enormous revival of interest in this idea. Digital technology now enables the pooling of opinions on a vast scale. Collectively we can rate products, predict futures, solve puzzles and even edit an encyclopedia better than any one of us could do on our own. The internet has also dramatically lowered the barriers to entry. To join a group decision there is no longer any need to gather in the market square. We can do little bits of joint decision-making in all sorts of different places: all it needs is a click here, a search there. Why shouldn't we harness these benefits in politics?

The answer takes us back to ancient Athens. Direct democracy is a very difficult form of politics to manage. It only succeeds under carefully controlled conditions. It requires all sorts of devices to clamp down on impulsive behaviour, including the threat of violence when necessary. It also takes a lot of hard work.

The networked world we now inhabit, shaped by the interests of vast new corporations, fuelled by our online addictions and riven with impulsive behaviour, does not suit that description. We haven't rediscovered either our appetite for hard political work or our taste for political violence. Why would we, when we can be so much more easily gratified in other ways?

But democracy is not dead yet. The Leviathan still has life left in it. Regaining control of the machine world remains possible.

How? Someone has to do the hard work of recapturing the power of digital technology for democratic politics. It won't happen on its own. One way it might happen would be for elected representatives to use their authority to support experiments in direct democracy. We can't recreate ancient Athens. But we can try to make democracy more responsive than it is at present.

It has started in some places. In Iceland, following the catastrophic failures of the 2008 crash, voters were offered the chance to crowd-source a new constitution, and in Reykjavik citizens have been given control over the city budget through online votes. Something similar is underway in San Francisco, where participatory budgeting has been tried in a number of neighbourhoods. In Stockholm, online voting is used to help pre-determine what politicians get to decide. Spain, Australia and Argentina all have 'Net' parties, whose members use digital tools to decide on party policy. In Italy Beppe Grillo's Five Star Movement crowd-sources many of its policies, for better or for worse. So do 'Pirate' parties around the world.

At the same time, digital technology can work for democracy by finding optimal solutions to technically complex issues. This needn't involve consulting the voters directly. Instead, politicians can use machine learning to make their own jobs easier by providing them with a means of pre-testing their options. At present most policy solutions are simply a wish list of things elected officials think might work. The test is whether the voters will stand for them. New technology has the potential to do the testing before the voters get their say, making it more likely that they will approve what they are offered in the end.

There is nothing remotely spontaneous about these ways of doing politics. Any form of digitally enhanced democracy is still going to be very hard work. The internet will not revive democratic politics by itself. It will have to be driven through the political system we already have. Only politics can rescue politics.

Unfortunately, the political system we have is just as likely to block these initiatives as to encourage them. Our politics remains tribal. For every potential solution, there will be a group of people ready to jeer, and a group of politicians ready to encourage them. Digital technology is liable to enhance tribalism even as it tries to rescue us from it.

Take some of the places now experimenting with direct democracy: San Francisco, Reykjavik, Stockholm. Well, they would, wouldn't they? E-democracy suits urban environments where tech-savvy citizens tend to gather. If it works in San Francisco, why not scale it up to the rest of the country? Because if it works in San Francisco, large parts of the rest of the US won't want to touch it. Texan politics is currently defined by a strong desire not to turn into California. It is the Californian definition of what works that alienates so many Texans.

One of the largest divides in twenty-first century Western democracy is produced by education. Whether or not someone went to college is a more significant determinant of how they are likely to vote than age, class or gender. That was true in the election of Trump, in the Brexit vote, and in the election of Macron. The educated are a tribe. They stick together. They may tell themselves that they do this because they have a better understanding of how the world works. But that's what makes them so alienating to the other side: they appear to mistake their tribalism for superior wisdom.

This is the fundamental problem with seeing technology as an enhancement to representative democracy. Politicians are not like doctors or other professionals. We do not simply look to them for guidance and help. We look for them to reflect who we are. Superior forms of knowledge get in the way of that.

On a visit to the US from Germany during the first decade of the last century, Max Weber asked a group of American workers why they kept voting for politicians who seemed barely qualified for the task and ended up letting them down. He got this answer: 'We spit on these "professionals", these officials. We despise them. But if the offices are filled by a trained, qualified class, such as you have in your country, it will be the officials who spit on us.'[63] That sentiment still animates representative democracy today.

The digital revolution promised much for democratic politics and so far has delivered little. Yet its transformative potential remains practically limitless. So now we have to face the hardest question of all. What if the thing that is getting in the way of a better politics is democracy itself? What then?

4

Something better?

CONTEMPORARY REPRESENTATIVE democracy is tired, vindictive, paranoid, self-deceiving, clumsy and frequently ineffectual. Much of the time it is living on past glories. This sorry state of affairs reflects what we have become. But current democracy is not who we are. It is just a system of government, which we built and we can replace. So why don't we replace it with something better?

Of course, there are reasons why we haven't thrown in the towel just yet. Democracy has served us well in the past and we would be much worse off now if we had abandoned it too soon. But clinging on too long could do as much harm as giving up too early. It could be even worse.

In truth, that description I've just given is only the polite version. There are far more brutal assessments floating around. For example, the British philosopher Nick Land believes that democracy will soon be the death of civilisation as we know it. He writes with dripping contempt for all of it: 'The democratic politician and the electorate are now bound together by a circuit of reciprocal incitement, in which each side drives the other to ever more shameless extremities of hooting, prancing cannibalism, until the only alternative to shouting is being eaten.'[64] Because democracy has given up trying to confront our cognitive biases, it is wholly unable to tame the consumerist madness that will ultimately consume us all. This is true zombie politics:

> Democracy, which both in theory and evident historical fact accentuates time-preference to the point of convulsive feeding-frenzy, is thus as close to a precise negation of civilization as anything could be, short of instantaneous social collapse into murderous barbarism or zombie apocalypse (which it eventually leads to). As the democratic virus burns through society, painstakingly accumulated habits and attitudes of forward-thinking, prudential, human and industrial investment, are replaced by a sterile, orgiastic consumerism, financial incontinence, and a 'reality television' political circus. Tomorrow might belong to the other team, so it's best to eat it all now.[65]

Never mind asking what might be better. It would be hard to imagine anything worse.

So what do writers like Land suggest as an alternative? This is where the problems start. Land would like to turn the democratic state into a vast corporation ('gov-corp'), with its own unelected CEO. Citizens become nothing more than customers. 'There is no longer any need for residents (clients) to take any interest in politics whatsoever. In fact, to do so would be to exhibit semi-criminal proclivities. If gov-corp doesn't deliver acceptable value for its taxes (sovereign rent), they can notify its customer service function, and if necessary take their custom elsewhere. Gov-corp would concentrate upon running an efficient, attractive, vital, clean, and secure country, of a kind that is able to draw customers. No voice, free exit.' Land believes that this offers the only alternative to the rule of what he calls 'the Cathedral', the shadowy organisation that is allegedly pushing nation states towards world government. 'The Cathedral' has as its creed the ideas emanating from 'the Grievance Studies departments of the New England universities'.

Land gets much of his philosophy – including the notion of 'the Cathedral' – from computer scientist Curtis Yarvin, who writes under the pseudonym Mencius Moldbug. Land and Yarvin are sometimes described as 'neo-reactionaries', but Yarvin says he prefers to be called a 'restorationist' or 'Jacobite'.[66] He means this literally. He would like to restore a form of absolute monarchy, on the grounds that modern politics took a wrong turn after 1688. Indeed, Yarvin rejects the phrase 'absolute monarch', which he considers a form of liberal sneering. He prefers simply to say 'monarch', any royal person capable of concentrating the decision-making power of the state in a single biological unit. Moldbug's favourite philosopher is Hobbes, but only before democracy got hold of his Leviathan.

How can we take these ideas seriously as an alternative? The most radical critics of contemporary democracy offer solutions that sound more like symptoms of what has gone wrong than any possible cure. Both Land and Yarvin are conspiracy theorists on a gargantuan scale. Their contempt for everything they dislike outweighs their capacity to describe anything plausible that might replace it. The political world they conjure up is a caricature, populated with incredible heroes and villains, which makes it impossible to believe in. This is true of many people who have given up on democracy. Their loathing for it leaves them unable to think about how it might turn into something else. They just want to get to the next stage as quickly as possible.

Alessio Piergiacomi, a software engineer at Amazon,

has written of the coming obsolescence of democracy. 'Year after year, the average person is becoming more stupid and the politicians more deceptive ... On the other hand, computers are becoming more intelligent every year ... Eventually it is going to be wiser to let them take the decisions and govern us.'[67] In response, a fellow engineer wrote: 'We already have a large number of people who are far better suited to run a country than our politicians. The people who run countries do so because they are good at playing the dirty game of politics. Once we create a robot who is capable of playing politics, and thus get elected, we will have a robot which is no better at running a country than our current politicians.'[68] It is hard to compete with cynicism like that. Or to know what could possibly come next.

The absence of plausible alternatives has long been one of the forces holding democracy in place. Widespread contemporary disgust with democratic politics is unmatched by any agreement about what would be better. Most of the alternatives sound a lot worse. Populism feeds off this imbalance: disliking democracy while having nothing to replace it with is the fuel for many conspiracy theories. It makes it far easier to persuade people they are being conned.

Churchill's celebrated remark about democracy reflects its enduring status as a lesser-evil kind of politics:

> Many forms of government have been tried and will be tried in this world of sin and woe. No one pretends that democracy is perfect or all wise. Indeed it has been said that democracy is the worst form of government except for all those other forms that have been tried from time to time.[69]

This line gets repeated ad nauseam in the twenty-first

century. None the less, context matters. Churchill was speaking in 1947, after the total failure of one catastrophic experiment with a possible alternative to democracy: fascism. Another experiment, Stalinism, was still ongoing. In the aftermath of the Second World War democracies knew that the chance to do something different was real and that it was extremely risky. The alternatives were tangible.

Seventy years later, the situation is different. Most democracies have grown used to thinking that there is no other option. Where radical experiments have been tried they often appear trivial or impossibly remote. What happens in the suburbs of Stockholm does not capture the imagination of people in Washington. Churchill was warning against temptations that could hardly have been more present. Now, it is more likely that we will miss realistic alternatives because we are so accustomed to thinking that they can't work. This is another function of democratic middle age. In younger democracies there is a sense that the future is open, for better or for worse. That feeling is lost in mature democracies. They get set in their ways.

There is little difference between thinking that there is no alternative and believing that the only alternatives are the outrageous ones. These states of mind go together: they are what produce the mid-life crisis. Yet there should be plenty of space between them, where it is possible to consider whether realistic alternatives do exist. The difficulty is finding it. One place to start is to try to work out what it was about democracy that attracted us in the first place. It ought to be part of the therapy.

The appeal of modern democracy is essentially twofold. First, it offers dignity. The individual inhabitants of democratic states have their views taken seriously by politicians. They get the chance to express them and they get protection when other people try to silence them. Democracy gives respect. Second, it delivers long-term benefits. Over time, living in a secure democratic state promises citizens a chance of sharing in the material advantages of stability, prosperity and peace. Each of these would be a significant attraction on its own. Taken together they are a formidable combination.

Inevitably, dignity will tend to come before long-term benefits. The appeal of being free to vote in an election is immediate. That is why it is common to see long queues at polling stations in democracies that have only just got off the ground and where any other advantages have yet to become apparent. Delivering results takes time. It is also true that democratic dignity tends to attach to individuals, whereas the long-term advantages are more diffuse.

To live in a democracy is to be given certain guarantees that you will be respected as a person, because every vote counts. Some of these are only paper guarantees and have to be fought for (this is especially true if you belong to a minority). But there is no guarantee that your personal fortunes will improve. Indeed, many individuals feel left out of the material benefits of democracy. The results delivered by democratic states are hard to pin down. They tend to come in the form of public goods. Getting them equitably distributed is also something that has to be fought for.

One of the ironies of democratic life is that elections, which are a big part of its appeal, do not reflect what is most appealing about it. Politicians pitching for votes will tell stories about the material advantages to the individual voter of this or that policy; at the same time, they appeal to notions of collective dignity. So, in some ways, the grounds of attraction are reversed: if you vote

for me, the candidate says, you will be better off personally and the group to which you belong will be better
respected. This is what makes democracy frustrating.
Its true appeal is a background condition against which
much more superficial appeals are made by politicians.

That gap – between what is promised to you as an
individual and what is provided to society as a whole
– leaves plenty of room for alternative offers. Some of
these alternatives are the ideological ones that were
tried and failed in the twentieth century. Marxism-
Leninism promised to collapse the distinction between
what's good for the individual and what's good for
society. Lenin, in *The State and Revolution*, argued that
true socialism would make personal life and political
life interchangeable. That way, there would be no need
for a police force or a state bureaucracy because the
people would be able to police and administer themselves. Lenin called this true democracy: the only
way to close the circle. He published these ideas just
before the Bolshevik revolution of 1917. The politics
that followed did not bear them out. Leninism became
Stalinism, which in turn became the drab and oppressive Soviet regime of the post-war era. In the long run,
representative democracy, for all its failings, is better
than that.

However, the alternatives do not have to be ideological. Twenty-first century authoritarianism is much
more pragmatic than its predecessors. Its practitioners
know that no one can close the circle, least of all ideologically driven politicians. Contemporary authoritarians have tried to learn the lessons of the twentieth
century like everyone else. They offer the other half
of what democracy can provide, but not the whole. In
place of personal dignity plus collective benefits, they
promise personal benefits plus collective dignity. This

is the essence of what the ruling Communist Party of China is currently committed to delivering.

Collective dignity comes in the form of national self-assertion: make China great again! Personal benefits are underwritten by the state, which does what it can to ensure that they are widely distributed. In recent decades non-democratic China has made greater progress in reducing poverty and raising life expectancy than democratic India. The immediate advantages of rapid economic growth are real for many Chinese citizens. The regime understands that its survival depends on this continuing for as long as possible.

There is a cost. Chinese citizens do not have the same opportunities for democratic self-expression as their Indian counterparts. Personal political dignity is harder to come by in a society that stifles freedom of speech and allows for the arbitrary exercise of power. A Chinese citizen is less likely than an Indian to suffer absolute poverty and its consequences – including malnutrition, illiteracy and early death – but more likely to suffer victimisation at the hands of an unaccountable state official. Collective political dignity – nationalism – is offered as some compensation. This will only work for individuals who belong to the majority national group. It does not help in Tibet.

At the same time, a reliance on the continuation of rapid economic growth comes with significant risks. The great long-term strength of modern democracies is their ability to change course when things go wrong. They are flexible. The danger of the pragmatic authoritarian alternative is that when the short-term benefits start to dry up, it may be difficult to find another basis for political legitimacy. Pragmatism may not be enough. The Chinese regime has yet to reach that point, so we do not know what will happen. If it fails to adapt, the downside of this form of politics will soon start to outweigh the benefits.

Pragmatic twenty-first century authoritarianism represents a real alternative to contemporary democracy. It offers a different sort of trade off. Which do we prefer: personal dignity or collective dignity? Short-term rewards or long-term benefits? These are serious questions. That said, the way modern democracy currently works makes it hard to tell whether anyone is taking them seriously. Trump shows why.

Trump's electoral pitch in 2016 came straight out of the pragmatic authoritarian playbook. He promised to deliver collective dignity – at least for the majority group of white Americans. Make America great again! Stop letting other people push us around! At the same time, he promised to provide short-term material benefits, regardless of what economists and other pointy-heads might say about the long-term costs. He would bring the jobs back! He would triple the growth rate! He would protect everyone's welfare benefits! All this made him sound like a typical twenty-first century authoritarian. But it also made him sound like a typical, if exceptionally brazen, democratic politician. He was making promises he couldn't keep.

It is difficult to believe that Trump's supporters were actually embracing the Chinese alternative to American democracy. Trump's behaviour in office has already given the lie to many of his campaign pledges. His pragmatism, such as it is, looks more improvisational than authoritarian. From what we know, the Chinese political elite views his rise with a mixture of anxiety and contempt. Trump has obscured the line between democracy and the alternatives. As with so much else, his election clarifies nothing.

So let's park Trump for the moment and return to the

bigger question. If pragmatic authoritarianism offers a genuine alternative to modern representative democracy, when would it make sense to choose it? It depends on where you are. For young democracies, especially if the arrival of democratic dignity has not yet been matched by tangible material benefits, pragmatic authoritarianism can be very attractive. The same is true for countries where democracy has not got going at all. We see this in many parts of the world today, where the Chinese model of government is winning converts. It is happening in Asia, in Africa, and even on the fringes of Europe. Chinese investment in these places has helped, but that is not the whole story. Rapid economic development, coupled with national self-assertion, has obvious appeal for states that need to deliver results in a relatively short period of time. In these places democracy often looks like the riskier bet.

Pragmatic authoritarianism can also have a strong pull in societies that face urgent environmental challenges. Perhaps the biggest international success of the Chinese state in the last decade has been to build a plausible case that it is capable of taking decisive action on climate change. Some of this is based on bold, imaginative gestures: doubling solar capacity in a single year (2016) or pledging to turn all Beijing's taxis into electric vehicles. It is a remarkable transformation from the smog of the post-Maoist era.

Pragmatic environmental authoritarianism can make democracy look cumbersome and indecisive by comparison. Democracies are good at keeping their options open but sometimes that means waiting until it's too late. When flooding or air pollution or water scarcity have become an acute threat, pragmatic authoritarianism has delivered on its promise to prioritise immediate results over long-term gains. It has much less to worry about when it comes to respecting the views of dissenters.

But that is not enough to tip the balance in mature democracies. There the trade-off works the other way. Human beings tend to suffer from loss aversion: we don't like to give up what we think is ours by right, regardless of the compensations on offer. It is very hard to imagine the citizens of Western democracies acquiescing in the loss of the personal dignity that comes with being able to kick the bastards out, even if it means bearing a collective material cost. We see plenty of evidence for this, too. Economic growth has been stagnant in much of western Europe for more than a decade. In the US, wages for many Americans have barely grown in real terms for more than forty years. The result is that voters have been drawn to politicians offering the promise of something different at election time. But they have not endorsed anyone threatening to take away their democratic rights. The authoritarian reflex has been limited to threats to take away the democratic rights of others: people who don't belong.

This is not an alternative to democracy. It is simply the populist distortion of it. Democratic authoritarians like the Hungarian leader Viktor Orban – who describes himself as an 'illiberal democrat' – take their inspiration from Vladimir Putin rather than the Chinese Communist Party. Pragmatism in countries like Hungary and Russia comes a distant second place to scapegoating and elaborate conspiracy theories. Elections still take place. Democracy is talked up, stripped of its liberal credentials. As a result, it is barely democracy at all – some political scientists prefer the label 'competitive authoritarianism' to describe what's going on.[70] The choice is there but it's an empty one. This is a parody of democracy rather than a replacement for it.

Chinese politics is hardly immune to scapegoating and conspiracy theories. Its leaders pose as strongmen.

But as a viable alternative to democracy, Beijing has something to offer that Moscow and Budapest can only gesture towards, just as Trump can only gesture towards it: practical results for the majority. The Chinese political system projects itself as meritocratic. Its politicians rise on the basis of a complex series of internal tests that value competence over charisma. Many in the West remain sceptical. In the words of Oxford historian Timothy Garton Ash, the system is still rife with 'factionalism, clientelism, patronage and corruption'.[71] Yet even Garton Ash admits that there has also been 'significant political reform and change … This is not a version of the Soviet Union.' Sinologist Daniel A. Bell calls the Chinese system 'democracy on the bottom, experimentation in the middle, meritocracy at the top'.[72] Even if there are good reasons to doubt the first and third parts of this description, the second still has a pull for Western observers. Aren't the Chinese at least trying to do something new?

Nevertheless, although mature democracies may flirt with pragmatic authoritarianism, they are unlikely to embrace it. The balance of risk favours tinkering with what they have over a bet on something different. Of course, circumstances may change. Extreme economic loss – or some other catastrophe, perhaps an environmental one – could fundamentally alter the terms of the trade-off. It is possible to imagine that a mature democracy would choose to throw in its lot with this alternative. But we are not there yet, not even close. The example of contemporary Greece makes this clear. An economic collapse on the scale of the 1930s has not been enough to persuade Greeks to give up on the dignity that comes with freedom of expression plus the long-run advantage of being able to chop and change political course in search of a way out of the mess. It remains a powerfully attractive combination for people who have lived with it for a while.

Churchill was therefore only half right. Democracy remains the least worst option for many of us, for now. But it is not the least worst option for everyone. There are realistic alternatives. The twenty-first century is likely to see Western democracy confronted by a rival political system whose appeal will vary from place to place and will occasionally stretch to include the edges of our politics. The temptations are real, even if the alternative is currently unrealistic for most Western societies. Democracy is no longer the only game in town.

Equally, we should recognise the limits in the trade-off we have chosen. The kind of respect provided by representative democracy may prove insufficient for twenty-first century citizens. The premium democracy places on personal dignity has traditionally been expressed through extensions to the franchise. Giving people the vote is the best way to let them know that they count. But when almost all adults are able to vote, we inevitably look for new ways to secure greater respect. The rise of identity politics is an indication that taking part in elections is not enough any more. Individuals are seeking the dignity that comes with being recognised for who they are. They don't just want to be listened to. They want to be *heard*. Social networks have provided a forum through which these demands can be voiced. Democratic politicians are struggling to know how to meet them.

The politics of recognition is an extension of democracy's appeal rather than a repudiation of it. Authoritarianism is no answer here, regardless of how pragmatic it is – it just results in political leaders who try to drown out demands for recognition with even louder demands of their own. You want respect? the authoritarian says. Then respect me! But representative democracy may not have the answers either. It is too mechanical to be convincing, once the stakes for respect get raised. Elected politicians increasingly tiptoe around the minefield of identity politics, unsure which way to turn, terrified of giving offence. If this continues, then the attraction that has held democracy together for so long will start to fray. Respect plus results is a fearsome combination. One without the other may not be enough.

However, this line of thought leads to a more radical possibility. If we can't continue to have personal respect plus good collective outcomes, perhaps we should pick between them. Maybe it is not a trade-off. Maybe it is a straightforward choice. If we insist that every voice counts, then we shouldn't be surprised that politics turns into a cacophonous mess. If we want the best results, perhaps we should limit political input to the people who know best how to achieve them.

Twenty-first century authoritarianism can provide a partial, pragmatic alternative to democracy. There is a more dogmatic alternative, which has its roots in the nineteenth century. Why not ditch the dignity that comes with voting altogether? Give up on personal respect – it's not worth it. Respect the experts instead!

Should we try it?

THE NAME FOR THIS VIEW of politics is epistocracy: the rule of the knowers. It is directly opposed to democracy, because it argues that the right to participate in political decision-making depends on whether you know what you are doing. The basic premise of democracy has always been that it doesn't matter if you know what you are doing, you get a say because you have to live with the consequences of what you do. In ancient Athens, this principle was reflected in the practice of choosing office-holders by lottery. Anyone could do it because everyone – well, anyone who wasn't a woman, a foreigner, a pauper, a slave or a child – counted as a member of the state. With the exception of jury service in some countries, we don't choose people at random for important roles any more. But we do uphold the underlying idea by letting citizens vote without checking their suitability for the task.

Critics of democracy – starting with Plato – have always argued that it means rule by the ignorant. Or worse, rule by the charlatans that the ignorant people fall for. Living in Cambridge, England, a passionately pro-European town and home to an elite university, I heard echoes of that argument in the aftermath of the Brexit vote. It was usually uttered sotto voce – you have to be a brave person to come out as an epistocrat in a democratic society – but it was unquestionably there. Behind their hands, very intelligent people muttered to each other that this is what you get if you ask a question that ordinary people don't understand. Dominic Cummings, the author of the 'Take Back Control' slogan that helped win the referendum, found that his critics were not so shy about spelling it out to his face. Brexit happened, they told him, because the wicked people lied to the stupid people. So much for democracy.

To say that democrats want to be ruled by the stupid and ignorant is unfair. No defender of democracy has ever claimed that stupidity or ignorance are virtues in themselves. But it is true that democracy doesn't discriminate on the grounds of lack of knowledge. It considers the ability to think intelligently about difficult questions a secondary consideration. The primary consideration is whether an individual is implicated in the outcome.

Democracy asks only that the voters should be around long enough to suffer for their own mistakes.

The question that epistocracy poses is: why don't we discriminate on the basis of knowledge? What's so special about letting everyone take part? Behind it lies the intuitively appealing thought that, instead of living with our mistakes, we should do everything in our power to prevent them in the first place. Then it wouldn't matter who has to take responsibility. This argument has been around for more than two thousand years. For most of that time it has been taken very seriously. The consensus until the end of the nineteenth century was that democracy is usually a bad idea: it is just too risky to put power in the hands of people who don't know what they are doing. Of course, that was only the consensus among intellectuals. We have little way of knowing what ordinary people thought about the question. Nobody was asking them.

Over the course of the twentieth century the intellectual consensus was turned around. Democracy established itself as the default condition of politics, its virtues far outweighing its weaknesses. Now the twenty-first century has revived some of the original doubts. Democracies do seem to be doing some fairly stupid things at present. Perhaps no one will be able to live with their mistakes. In the age of Trump and Modi, climate change and nuclear weapons, epistocracy has teeth again.

So why don't we give more weight to the views of the people who are best qualified to evaluate what to do? Before answering that question, it is important to distinguish between epistocracy and something with which it is often confused: technocracy. They are different. Epistocracy means rule by the people who know best. Technocracy is rule by mechanics and engineers. A technocrat is someone who understands how the machinery works.

The 2011 suspension of Greek democracy, for example, was an experiment in technocracy, not epistocracy. The engineers in this case were economists. Even highly qualified economists often haven't a clue what's best to do. What they know is how to operate a complex system they have been instrumental in building, so long as it behaves the way it is meant to. Technocrats are the people who understand what's best for the machine. But keeping the machine running may be the worst thing we can do. A technocrat won't help with that question.

Both representative democracy and Chinese-style pragmatic authoritarianism have plenty of space for technocracy. Increasingly, each system has put decision-making capacity in the hands of specially trained experts, particularly when it comes to economic questions. Central bankers wield significant power in a wide variety of political systems around the world. For that reason, technocracy is not really an alternative to democracy. Like populism, it is more of an add-on. What makes epistocracy different is that it prioritises the 'right' decision over the technically correct decision. It tries to work out where we should be going. A technocrat can only tell us how we should get there.

How would epistocracy function in practice? The obvious difficulty is knowing who should count as the knowers. There is no formal qualification for being a general expert. It is much easier to identify a suitable technocrat. Technocracy is more like plumbing than philosophy. When Greece went looking for economic experts to sort out its financial mess, it headed to Goldman Sachs and the other big banks, since that is where the technicians were congregated. When a machine goes wrong, the people responsible for fixing it often have their fingerprints all over it already.

Historically, some epistocrats have tackled the

problem of identifying who knows best by advocating non-technical qualifications for politics. If there were such a thing as the university of life, that's where these epistocrats would want political decision-makers to get their higher degrees. But since there is no such university, they often have to make do with cruder tests of competence. The nineteenth-century philosopher John Stuart Mill argued for a voting system that granted varying numbers of votes to different classes of people depending on what jobs they did.[73] Professionals and other highly educated individuals would get six or more votes each; farmers and traders would get three or four; skilled labourers would get two; unskilled labourers would get one. Mill also pushed hard for women to get the vote, at a time when that was a deeply unfashionable view. He did not do this because he thought women were the equals of men. It was because he thought some women, especially the better educated, were superior to most men. Mill was a big fan of discrimination, so long as it was on the right grounds.

To twenty-first century eyes, Mill's system looks grossly undemocratic. Why should a lawyer get more votes than a labourer? Mill's answer would be to turn the question on its head: why should a labourer get the same number of votes as a lawyer? Mill was no simple democrat, but he was no technocrat either. Lawyers didn't qualify for their extra votes because politics placed a special premium on legal expertise. No, lawyers got their extra votes because what's needed are people who have shown an aptitude for thinking about questions with no easy answers. Mill was trying to stack the system to ensure as many different points of view as possible were represented. A government made up exclusively of economists or legal experts would have horrified him. The labourer still gets a vote. Skilled labourers get two. But even though a task like brick-laying is a skill, it is a narrow one. What was needed was breadth. Mill believed that some points of view carried more weight simply because they had been exposed to more complexity along the way.

Jason Brennan, a very twenty-first century philosopher, has tried to revive the epistocratic conception of politics, drawing on thinkers like Mill. In his 2016 book *Against Democracy*, Brennan insists that many political questions are simply too complex for most voters to comprehend. Worse, the voters are ignorant about how little they know: they lack the ability to judge complexity because they are so attached to simplistic solutions that feel right to them. Brennan writes:

> Suppose the United States had a referendum on whether to allow significantly more immigrants into the country. Knowing whether this is a good idea requires tremendous social scientific knowledge. One needs to know how immigration tends to affect crime rates, domestic wages, immigrants' welfare, economic growth, tax revenues, welfare expenditures and the like. Most Americans lack this knowledge; in fact, our evidence is that they are systematically mistaken.[74]

In other words, it's not just that they don't know; it's not even that they don't know they don't know; it's that they are wrong in ways that reflect their unwavering belief that they are right.

Brennan doesn't have Mill's faith that we can tell how well equipped someone is to tackle a complex question by how difficult that person's job is. There is too much chance and social conditioning involved. He would prefer an actual exam, to 'screen out citizens who are badly misinformed or ignorant about the election, or who lack basic social scientific knowledge'.[75] Of course, this just pushes the fundamental problem back a stage without resolving it: who gets to set the exam? Brennan teaches in a university, so he has little faith in the disinterested qualities of most social scientists, who have their own ideologies and incentives. He has also seen students cramming for exams, which can produce its own biases and blind spots. Still, he thinks Mill was right to suggest that the further one advances up the educational ladder, the more votes one should get: five extra votes for finishing high school, another five for a bachelor's degree, and five more for a graduate degree.

Brennan is under no illusions about how provocative this case is one hundred and fifty years after Mill made it. In the middle of the nineteenth century, the idea that political status should track social and educational standing was barely contentious; today, it is barely credible. Brennan also has to face the fact that contemporary social science provides plenty of evidence that the educated are just as subject to groupthink as other people, sometimes even more so. The political scientists Larry Bartels and Christopher Achen point this out in their 2016 book *Democracy for Realists*: 'The historical record leaves little doubt that the educated, including the highly educated, have gone wrong in their moral and political thinking as often as everyone else.'[76] Cognitive biases are no respecters of academic qualifications. How many social science graduates would judge the question about immigration according to the demanding tests Brennan lays out, rather than according to what they would prefer to believe? The irony is that if Brennan's voter exam were to ask whether the better educated deserve more votes, the technically correct answer might be no. It would depend on who was marking it.

However, in one respect Brennan insists that the case for epistocracy has grown far stronger since Mill made it. That is because Mill was writing at the dawn of democracy. Mill published his arguments in the run-up to what became the Second Reform Act of 1867, which doubled the size of the franchise in Britain to nearly 2.5 million voters (out of a general population of 30 million). Mill's case for epistocracy was based on his conviction that over time it would merge into democracy. The labourer who gets one vote today would get more tomorrow, once he had learned how to use his vote wisely. Mill was a great believer in the educative power of democratic participation.

Brennan thinks we now have one hundred-plus years of evidence that Mill was wrong. Voting is bad for us. It doesn't make people better informed. If anything, it makes them stupider, because it dignifies their prejudices and ignorance in the name of democracy. 'Political participation is not valuable for most people,' Brennan writes. 'On the contrary, it does most of us little good and instead tends to stultify and corrupt us. It turns us into civic enemies who have grounds to hate one another.'[77] The trouble with democracy is that it gives us no reason to become better informed. It tells us we are fine as we are. And we're not.

In the end, Brennan's argument is more historical than philosophical. If we were unaware of how democracy would turn out, it might make sense to cross our fingers and assume the best of it. But he insists that we do know. So we have no excuse to keep kidding ourselves. Brennan thinks that we should regard epistocrats like himself as being in the same position as democrats were in the mid-nineteenth century. What he is championing is anathema to many people, as democracy was back then. Still, we took a chance on democracy, waiting to see how it would turn out. Why shouldn't we take a chance on epistocracy, now we know how the other experiment went? Why do we assume that democracy is the only experiment we are ever allowed to run, even after it has run out of steam?

It's a serious question, and it gets to how the longevity of democracy has stifled our ability to think about the possibility of something different. What was once a seemingly reckless form of politics has become a byword for caution. And yet there are still good reasons to be cautious about ditching it. Epistocracy remains the reckless idea. There are two dangers in particular.

The first is that we set the bar too high in politics by insisting we look for the best thing to do. Sometimes it is more important to avoid the worst. Even if democracy is often bad at coming up with the right answers, it is good at unpicking the wrong ones. Moreover, it is good at exposing people who think they always know best. Democratic politics assumes there is no settled answer to any question and it ensures that is the case by allowing everyone a vote, including the ignorant. The randomness of democracy – which remains its essential quality – protects us against getting stuck with truly bad ideas. It means that nothing will last for long, because something else will come along to disrupt it.

Epistocracy is flawed because of the second part of the word rather than the first – this is about power ('*kratos*') as much as it is about knowledge ('*episteme*'). Fixing power to knowledge risks creating a monster that can't be deflected from its course, even when it goes wrong – which it will, since no one and nothing is infallible. Not knowing the right answer is a great defence against people who believe that their knowledge makes them superior.

Brennan's response to this argument (a version of which is made by David Estlund in his 2007 book *Democratic Authority*) is to turn it on its head.[78] Since democracy is a form of *kratos*, too, he says, why aren't we concerned to protect individuals from the incompetence of the *demos* just as much as from the arrogance of the epistocrats? But these are not the same kinds of power. Ignorance and foolishness don't oppress in the same way that knowledge and wisdom do, precisely because they are incompetent: the demos keeps changing its mind.

The democratic case against epistocracy is a version of the democratic case against pragmatic authoritarianism. You have to ask yourself where you'd rather be when things go wrong. Maybe things will go wrong quicker and more often in a democracy, but that is a different issue. Rather than thinking of democracy as the least worst form of politics, we could think of it as the best when at its worst. It is the difference between Churchill's dictum and a similar one from Tocqueville a hundred years earlier that is less well-known but more apposite. More fires get started in a democracy, Tocqueville said, but more fires get put out, too.

The recklessness of epistocracy is also a function of the historical record that Brennan uses to defend it. One hundred-plus years of democracy may have uncovered its failings but they have also taught us that we can live with them. We are used to the mess and attached to the benefits. Being an epistocrat like Mill before democracy had got going is very different from being one once democracy is well established. We now know what we know, not just about democracy's failings, but about our tolerance for its incompetences.

Weber, writing at the turn of the twentieth century, took it for granted that universal suffrage was a dangerous idea, because of the way that it empowered the mindless masses. But he argued that once it had been granted, no sane politician should ever think about taking it away:

the backlash would be too terrible. The only thing worse than letting everyone vote is telling some people that they no longer qualify. Never mind who sets the exam, who is going to tell us that we've failed? Mill was right: democracy comes after epistocracy, not before. You can't run the experiment in reverse.

The cognitive biases that epistocracy is meant to rescue us from are what will ultimately scupper it. Loss aversion makes it more painful to be deprived of something we have that doesn't always work than something we don't have that might. It's like the old joke. Q: 'Do you know the way to Dublin?' A: 'Well, I wouldn't start from here.' How do we get to a better politics? Well, maybe we shouldn't start from here. But here is where we are.

That said, there must be other ways of trying to inject more wisdom into democratic politics than an exam. This is the twenty-first century: we have new tools to work with. If many of the problems with democracy derive from the business of politicians hawking for votes at election time, which feeds noise and bile into the decision-making process, perhaps we should try to simulate what people would choose under more sedate and reflective conditions. For instance, it may be possible to extrapolate from what is known about voters' interests and preferences what they ought to want if they were better able to access the knowledge they needed. We could run mock elections that replicate the input from different points of view, as happens in real elections, but which strip out all the distractions and distortions of democracy in action. Brennan suggests the following:

> We can administer surveys that track citizens' political preferences and demographic characteristics, while testing their basic objective political knowledge.

Once we have this information, we can simulate what would happen if the electorate's demographics remained unchanged, but all citizens were able to get perfect scores on tests of objective political knowledge. We can determine, with a strong degree of confidence, what 'We the People' would want if only 'We the People' understood what we were talking about.[79]

Democratic dignity goes out the window under such a system – we are each reduced to data points in a machine-learning exercise. But the outcomes should improve.

In 2017 a US-based digital technology company called Kimera Systems announced that it was close to developing an AI named Nigel, whose job was to help voters know how they should vote in an election, based on what it already knew of their personal preferences. Its creator, Mounir Shita, declared: 'Nigel tries to figure out your goals and what reality looks like to you and is constantly assimilating paths to the future to reach your goals. It's constantly trying to push you in the right direction.'[80] This is the more personalised version of what Brennan is proposing, with some of the democratic dignity plugged back in. Nigel is not trying to work out what's best for everyone, only what's best for you. It accepts your version of reality. Yet Nigel understands that you are incapable of drawing the correct political inferences from your preferences. You need help, from a machine that has seen enough of your personal behaviour to understand what it is you are after. Siri recommends books you might like. Nigel recommends political parties and policy positions.

Would this be so bad? To many people it instinctively sounds like a parody of democracy because it treats us like confused children. Yet to Shita it is an enhancement of democracy because it takes our desires seriously. Democratic politicians don't much care what it is that we actually want. They care what it is they can persuade us we want, so they can better appeal to it. Nigel puts the voter first. At the same time, by protecting us from our own confusion and inattention, Nigel strives to improve our self-understanding. Brennan's version effectively gives up on Mill's original idea that voting might be an educative experience. Shita hasn't given up. Nigel is trying to nudge us along the path to self-knowledge. We might end up learning who we really are.

The fatal flaw with this approach, however, is that we risk learning only who it is we think we are, or who it is we would like to be. Worse, it is who we would like to be now, not who or what we might become in the future. Like focus groups, Nigel provides a snapshot of a set of attitudes at a moment in time. The danger of any system of machine learning is that it produces feedback loops. By restricting the data set to our past behaviour, Nigel teaches us nothing about what other people think or even about other ways of seeing the world. Nigel simply mines the archive of our attitudes for the most consistent expression of our identities. If we lean left, we will end up leaning more left. If we lean right, we will end up leaning more right. Social and political division would widen. Nigel is designed to close the circle in our minds.

There are technical fixes for feedback loops. Systems can be adjusted to inject alternative points of view, to notice when data is becoming self-reinforcing or simply to randomise the evidence. We can shake things up to lessen the risk that we get set in our ways. For instance, Nigel could make sure that we visit websites that challenge rather than reinforce our preferences. Alternatively, on Brennan's model, the aggregation of our preferences could seek to take account of the likelihood that Nigel had exaggerated rather than tempered who we really are. A Nigel of Nigels – a machine that helps other machines to better align their own goals – may try to strip out the distortions from the artificial democracy we have built. After all, Nigel is our servant, not our master. We can always tell him what to do.

But that is the other fundamental problem with twenty-first century epistocracy. We won't be the ones telling Nigel what to do. It will be the technicians who have built the system. They are the experts we rely on to rescue us from feedback loops. For this reason it is hard to see how twenty-first century epistocracy can avoid collapsing back into technocracy. When things go wrong, the knowers will be powerless to correct for them. Only the engineers who built the machines have that capacity, which means that it will be the engineers who have the power.

History teaches us that epistocracy comes before democracy. It can't come after. What comes next down this road is technocracy, which is not an alternative to democracy. It is simply a distortion of it.

THERE IS ANOTHER WAY TO GO. If we return to the choice that led down the path to epistocracy, we could try taking the other fork instead. Inputs or outputs? Respect or results? Why not give up on searching for the best outcomes and focus instead on ensuring that everyone gets to do their own thing. To hell with the consequences.

Many contemporary critics of democracy believe that it is the fixation on results that has left us stuck where we are. We are terrified of doing anything different because we are so frightened of making things worse. Technocracy feeds off the fear that system failure is the worst thing that could happen. Is it really? What if the endless pursuit of marginally better outcomes – more economic growth, longer lives, higher educational standards – is blinding us to the possibility of real political and social change?

Take economic growth. There is strong historical evidence that when the economy stalls, democracy fractures. From the 1890s to the 2010s, the absence of economic growth has repeatedly fuelled the rise of populist anger. Voters need a sense that the future will be materially better than the past if they are to resist the appeal of politicians who tell them that the present is the fault of someone else. The economist Benjamin Friedman has made this case most forcefully: the reason growth matters is not for its own sake, but because the healthy functioning of democracy depends on it.[81] Yet there is a treadmill quality to that argument. We need growth to keep democracy moving, so we orient our democracy around the politics of growth. Could we step off even if we wanted to?

Liberation may depend on being willing to risk failure by these standards. We could stop trying to take care of all the tasks that have been accumulated by democratic politicians over the last century. We could let people decide for themselves what matters, even if that ignores the conventional imperatives of political stability. We could give up on insisting that democracy only functions when the hierarchy works with the network. We could set the networks free.

The extreme version of this position is anarchism: the idea that no one should ever be subject to the power of another. Anarchism makes collective outcomes irrelevant – all that count are the decisions that individuals take for themselves. The possibility of anarchy hovers in the background of every form of politics, democracy included. It is rarely more than a passing fantasy. But when democracy has grown stale and dispiriting it has increasing appeal. Twenty-first century anarchism flourishes online, where freedom of choice is rampant. It also flowers occasionally on the streets, at protests like Occupy Wall Street. Yet as a practical means of organising contemporary societies it is not really an alternative to democracy. It is an alternative to organised politics altogether. That is too much for most people.

There are political alternatives. Digital technology has opened up the possibility that a world of self-sustaining networks need not be entirely anarchic. It would require politics to operate on two different levels. There has to be an overarching framework, which creates the conditions for political experimentation to take place without prejudging the outcomes. And then there are the political experiments themselves. The internet could be the framework. The political experiments could be anything.

This idea has appeal at both ends of the political spectrum. For those on the right, it taps into a libertarian tradition that says the state should never be more than a neutral watchman, doing the minimum needed to keep us safe from each other but leaving everything else up for grabs. The classic 1970s description of this view was provided by Robert Nozick in *Anarchy, State, and Utopia* (1974), a book that still has a wide readership in Silicon Valley. The best-known parts of the argument are where Nozick makes the case against the redistribution of wealth through the tax system, which he equates to a form of slavery. That's why rich people like the book. But the most interesting part is the final section ('Utopia'), where Nozick argues that a minimal state leaves open all the important questions for individuals to decide for themselves. What kind of society do you want to live in? Who do you want to share it with? These are not matters to be settled by politics. These are things politics should leave up to us.

Nozick makes his point with a list:

> Wittgenstein, Elizabeth Taylor, Bertrand Russell, Thomas Merton, Yogi Berra, Allen Ginsberg, Harry Wolfson, Thoreau, Casey Stengel, The Lubbavitcher Rebbe, Picasso, Moses, Einstein, Hugh Hefner, Socrates, Henry Ford, Lenny Bruce, Baba Ram Das, Gandhi, Sir Edmund Hillary, Raymond Lubitz, Buddha, Frank Sinatra, Columbus, Freud, Norman Mailer, Ayn Rand, Baron Rothschild, Ted Williams, Thomas Edison, H. L. Mencken, Thomas Jefferson, Ralph Ellison, Bobby Fischer, Emma Goldman, Peter Kropotkin, you and your parents: Is there really one kind of life that is right for all these people?[82]

Nozick thinks the mistake utopians make is to assume that their idealised society will work for everyone. No matter how it works or who designs it, some people are bound to loathe it. Instead, we should recognise that the best society would be one in which different human types can find their own way to live. Communism would only be utopia for the people who prefer things that way; for others it would be hell. The same is true for Gandhi's asceticism, for Emma Goldman's anarchism and even Ayn Rand's version of libertarianism, which trumpets the virtues of the free market. Nozick thinks a true utopia would need to have room for all these things, and to allow them to be freely chosen by the different people who lived there.

The internet makes that utopia something like a real possibility. All sorts of freely formed communities flourish in the digital age. Though these include many anarchist groups, it is not anarchy overall because there are also rules, set by the architects of the system. In practice, these rules are not neutral because they currently reflect the interests of the giant technology companies and of the states that are trying to regulate them. But in theory they could be neutral. The internet certainly has room for multiple different visions of the good life to co-exist.

Nozick's list would need to be updated for the twenty-first century (here's mine, though really it could be anyone's): 'Rihanna, Ai Weiwei, Margaret Atwood, Travis Kalanick, Maria Sharapova, PSY, Janet Yellen, Russell Brand, Larry David, J. K. Rowling, Pope Francis, Lena Dunham, Mohammed al-Zawahiri, Kid Rock, etc., etc.' In fact, what's most dated about Nozick's litany of names (apart from the fact that they are almost all men) is the assumption that someone needs to be famous to have a vision of the good life we can recognise. In the 1970s there was little opportunity for anybody without name recognition to project their views about how they wished to live: only the lucky few could find an audience. Digital technology has the potential to liberate the inner utopian in all of us. In practice, again, it hasn't really happened like that. Celebrity dominates more than ever, as we congregate online around the Instagram feeds of the famous. But it is possible to imagine a world in which individuals can gather together in the political groupings that suit their personal preferences, rather than according the accidents of their geographical locations or the siren call of celebrity. That, as Nozick would say, is the true utopia.

The left variant on this idea is similar but different. The similarity is a conviction that the internet can rescue individuals from the arbitrary hold of the political systems in which they happen to find themselves. The difference is that the oppressor to be overcome is not the redistributive state but the capitalist free market. Left liberationists want to find the escape route from money power.

Paul Mason, in his 2015 book *Postcapitalism*, writes about the emancipatory potential of information technology with the zeal of a true libertarian. 'With the rise of the networks,' he says, 'the capacity for meaningful action is no longer confined to states, corporations and political parties; individuals and temporary swarms of individuals can be just as powerful agents of change.'[83] The ground of Mason's belief in this change, however, is Marxist.

Marx is best known for the idea that capitalism exploits labour, to the point where the only way out is a revolution by the workers. But there is another possible pathway to emancipation. Mason finds it in a relatively obscure text by Marx called 'The Fragment on Machines'. He summarises its argument as follows:

> In an economy where machines do most of the work, where human labour is really about supervising, mending and designing the machines, the nature of the knowledge locked inside the machines must be 'social'.[84]

This knowledge is much harder for capitalists to exploit, because in the end it does not belong to anyone. It belongs to everyone, which is what makes it 'social', so long as everyone has access to the machines that contain it.

Digital technology has made information rather than labour the primary commodity in our societies. As a result, we now have the potential to emancipate ourselves from the need to work for a living. Once the machines do the work for us, people can decide for themselves how they want to live. Marx had no idea how this might actually happen. He was writing in 1857. At the same time, Mason believes, he saw it coming.

Mason recognises the utopian strain in this way of thinking. The Marx-was-right-after-all rhetoric will put many readers off. Haven't we heard that one too many times before? But there are non-Marxist variants on the same line of thought. In *Pax Technica* (2015), a much less bombastic book than Mason's, Philip N. Howard argues that the 'internet of things' – whereby machines come to share vast quantities of data directly with each other – will entirely transform contemporary politics. Once your fridge can talk to your light bulb, we will be in a different political world, whether we like it or not. A lot of decisions will be out of our hands because machines will be taking them for us, in the name of greater efficiency. However, if machines are doing the hard work of connecting us together, that leaves human beings freer to play around. Machine learning might create new slack in the system, which is where human imagination can come back into politics.

Howard makes this case:

> We have to fundamentally change the way we think of
> political units and order. Digital media have changed
> the way we use our social networks and allowed
> us to be political actors when we choose to be. We
> use technology to connect to one another and to
> share stories. The state, the political party, the civic
> group, the citizen: these are all old categories from a
> pre-digital world ... The agency of the individual is
> being enhanced by the device networks of the internet
> of things.[85]

Howard is no revolutionary firebrand. He envisages two levels of politics in the future. On the one hand there needs to be agreement on the technical standards that govern the internet, which will inevitably be shaped by engineers and technology companies. On the other hand there are the networks that already exist on the internet, where people do things for themselves. This renders government as conventionally understood increasingly obsolete. It leaves technical governance on one side and direct political action on the other. There is little need for anything in between.

This 'pax technica' comes after the 'pax Americana', when one very powerful state was needed to keep the world at peace. That era seems to be over anyway, thanks to Trump. Howard thinks we will do fine without it. 'The internet of things,' he writes, 'will probably strengthen social cohesion to such a degree that when regular government structures break down or weaken, they can be repaired or substituted. In other words, people will continue using the internet of things to provide governance even when government is absent.' [86]

Libertarian, revolutionary or technocratic, these visions of the future have some features in common. One is their impatience to get there. Peter Thiel, the poster boy for Silicon Valley libertarianism, supported Trump for president because he wanted to shake things up. Thiel believes that all disruption is welcome – regardless of the consequences – because it brings the future just that little bit closer. Susan Sarandon, who became a spokesperson for Hollywood-style socialism, was of a similar view in 2016. Get Hillary and all you're left with is more of the same; get Trump and there's a chance that everything will give way at once.

A common refrain from these impatient visionaries is that we are worrying about the wrong things. We are fearful of disruption. We ought to welcome it. Instead of trying to avoid a leap into the unknown, we should recognise it as the precondition of meaningful change. Paul Mason writes that in the short term the aim of contemporary politics should be 'not to reduce complexity ... but to promote the most complex form of capitalist finance compatible with progressing the economy towards high automation, low work and abundant cheap or free goods and services'.[87] Capitalism needs to get to where it's going as quickly as possible because it is building the machines that will set us free. If we want a political motto for the twenty-first century, here it is: *speed up!*

This view of the world has acquired its own philosophical label: accelerationism. It had an early twentieth-century forerunner in futurism, which flourished in the period just before and after the First World War. Futurism was a philosophy that celebrated speed, mechanisation and youth. It was pretty relaxed about the violence that came along with them. Its proponents, especially in Italy, had a taste for first-generation motorbikes and they were equally relaxed about crashing them. Italian futurism did not end well. In 1919 the Partito Politica Futurista merged with Mussolini's newly formed fascists. The two movements discovered that they shared many of the same interests. A love of clean lines and a disregard for the effects of achieving them makes for bad politics.

Having already insisted that the twentieth century is not our guide to the present, I can hardly argue that the fate of futurism tells us where accelerationism will end up. Trump may be a spluttering, fat motorbike but the internet is something else altogether. It has very few clean lines and contains almost limitless complexity. We are not going back to the 1920s. Futurism belongs to the past.

Twenty-first century accelerationism is an economic philosophy as much as it is an aesthetic one. Its proponents dislike hair-shirt reactions to the present state of the world. Many environmentalists insist that we should cut back on our consumption, slow down what we do and value what we already have. Accelerationists think that would be a kind of suicide. They want us to embrace rapid economic growth, not for its own sake, and certainly not for the sake of preserving the political system we currently have. Rather, growth is the precondition of change. Grow fast enough and, in the words of one accelerationist manifesto, 'the future will crack right open'.[88]

Accelerationists have been criticised in the past for overestimating what is possible. The future rarely arrives as quickly as we think. Machines have traditionally only been as good as the people operating them and people don't change nearly as fast as machines do. The fate of futurism showed that. But the digital revolution may have altered the terms of the argument. The internet of things plays such a big role in accelerationist visions of the future because it promises to liberate machines from humans as much as humans from machines. It allows change to happen at the speed the machines can cope with. All the humans have to do is take advantage of what the machines have made possible. We don't have to change. We just have to get on board for the ride.

For that reason, the real danger may be that we overshoot rather than undershoot where we think we are going. Most utopian conceptions of a world of liberated networks assume that the individuals who constitute these networks will remain intact. We still get to choose how we want to co-exist, and with whom, in the limitless landscape that the internet has opened up. But it is possible that this landscape will prove deeply inhospitable to individual human identity.

Instead of individuals choosing where they belong,

the machines may refuse to recognise that we exist as individuals at all. We are simply collections of data points, and as the data gets parcelled out across the vast terrain of the internet, we get thinned out with it. When our fridge starts talking to our light bulb, without any conscious input from us, what are we to them except a credit card and a set of incoherent attitudes? As the Israeli historian Yuval Noah Harari terms it, the digital revolution threatens to 'de-individuate' us all.[89]

That would certainly put paid to Nozick's utopia, even the updated version. The libertarian paradise rests on the basic modern assumption that it is possible to put a name to the people we are so that we can choose how we want to live. That may not be true any more. What if I am not me, Rihanna is not Rihanna, Gandhi is not Gandhi, and there is no community that makes sense for any of us? Instead, different bits of us belong in different places. We each contain multitudes, and the machines see only the bits, not the whole. Once 'de-individuated' I won't be able to choose my preferred way of life because there will be nothing left of me to choose. There will only be the information I supply to the machines.

Perhaps that sounds implausible or defeatist. But implausibility is no argument against accelerationism. Its whole point is to get us used to the idea that the future may be nothing like what we expect. It is uncharted territory. Utopias used to be impossibly remote places where we had never been. Now there is a risk they become the places we speed by on our way to somewhere else. We glimpse them in passing. They do not have time to come into focus. Then they disappear from view.

Many accelerationists would happily embrace the idea that we will overshoot our final destination. They insist there is no such thing as a final destination anyway.

There is only the trip. Sooner or later we will have to take a leap in the dark. Eventually, perhaps within only a few decades, the categories of human and machine will blur. Then we will arrive at what gets called the Singularity: the point when the pace of change becomes unimaginable to the people we are today. After that, anything is possible.

Before that, however, we have to think about what might happen to the people we are now. There is a case to be made that some disaggregation of individual identity would be good for us. Derek Parfit has argued that our attachment to the illusion of a single identity over time is one of the things that stifles our moral and political imaginations.[90] We instinctively believe that we have more in common with the person we will be in twenty years' time than with the person sitting next to us right now. Parfit thinks that is wrong: we are as disconnected from our future selves as if there were physical space between us. I am not the me I will be in future. The two of us are essentially separate people.

If only we could see that, we might start to reconfigure our moral priorities. First, we would be more solicitous of our neighbours and of people further away, given the time we currently spend worrying only about ourselves. Second, we would do more to guard against doing harm to people who don't yet exist (for example, by squandering natural resources). If it is wrong to hurt the person sitting next to me, it is also wrong to hurt my or your future self. Disaggregated personhood should make us better and more responsible people than we are at present.

So far, there is little sign that information technology is having this effect. Parfit was writing in the mid-1980s, before the digital revolution had got going. His arguments assumed a backdrop of relative political stability: under conditions of calm philosophical reflection we should be able to see the things we owe to each other and to our future selves. In other words: first we stabilise, then we take our identities apart, then we put our moral universe back together again. At the moment that process is being played out in reverse: first we take our identities apart, then we destabilise, then we see what if anything is left of the moral universe we built. Our personalities are getting fractured in little ways, piece by piece – health data over here, WhatsApp over there, Twitter chattering away in the background – without anything to give us a shared perspective on what's happening. This is not taking place in a philosophy seminar. It is lived human experience, which makes calm reflection almost impossible. For now, technology is fraying us more than it is liberating us.

Parfit also assumed relative equality between individual human beings as a precondition of moral renewal: we will be able see what we truly owe each other once we can see each other as equals. By contrast, the fracturing effect of digital technology coincides with growing inequality. This is not simply the material inequality that comes with the capture of vast amounts of wealth by the titans of the digital world. It is the basic inequality that comes with some people being in closer touch with the machines than others. If you have access to the keys that control the system that controls our lives and I don't, then you and I will never be equals.

Hobbes's vision of politics, which prefigures the modern world, starts from the premise of equality. We need the state because we are naturally equal and therefore equally vulnerable to each other. The basic fact about human existence is that just about anyone can kill anyone else, given a weapon and the element of surprise. The Leviathan is practically impossible to kill, which gives it the power to put an end to the spiral of violence. It cannot abolish death, but it can set the terms that make a natural death more likely than an unnatural one. The reason most people today die of old age is because the state has come to protect them from other, more violent fates.

This natural equality may soon be a thing of the past. Technological transformation opens up the possibility that some people will try to buck death without any help from the Leviathan. It will be, to start with, only the hyper-privileged few who can afford to experiment with futuristic medical treatments that promise to reverse the ageing process. Even if most of these experiments fail, the possibility is still there that some might succeed. Vastly extended human life spans, and hugely unequal life prospects, undermine the rationale of modern politics. A few super-humans is all it would take to change entirely the basis on which we organise our societies. They would stand outside the rules of relative vulnerability that bind the rest of us. Knowledge in the information age is not just power. It has the potential to become a kind of superpower, which transcends politics.

The appetite to live for ever shows how distant we are from Parfit's vision of a world of selfless disaggregated selves. Particularly in Silicon Valley, the very wealthy do not see why they ever have to stop being themselves. Having made vast amounts of money, often at a ridiculously young age, they regard the future as their playground. And they are determined to be the people who get to play in it. As always, this is dressed up as a universal vision: death ought to be optional for everyone. But what that really means is that the most powerful people in the world want death to be optional for them. Otherwise, how can they get to enjoy the things that they are building?

If an accelerated future could be anything, we have to include the possibility that it will be a parody of the distant past. Strip out natural equality and the modern age becomes an interlude between eras of pharaonic excess. A few human beings flirt with immortality. Everyone else lives in their shadow. I said in the last chapter that pharaohs are no match for the power of the modern state. But without the modern state, we are no match for the pharaohs. If we take our politics apart, it will not be there to rescue us when we take ourselves apart, too.

I have considered three alternatives to modern democracy: pragmatic authoritarianism, epistocracy and liberated technology. The first two have things to recommend them, but in the end they don't stack up against the democracy we have, even in its parlous current state. They remain temptations rather than alternatives. The third is different. It includes all sorts of potential futures: some wondrous, some terrible, and most wholly unknowable. It is a spectrum of possibility, as wide as any human experience has ever known.

So it is certainly true that there are better options than contemporary democracy. The most attractive imagined futures include ways of doing politics that are an unambiguous improvement on what we have now. The best-case scenario under Howard's 'pax technica', for example, would combine global peace with personal liberation and increasing prosperity. That would be as good as anything we have known before. Mason thinks we can go much further, towards a world where all the best things in life are free. These are not simply utopian visions. They originate with things that are already happening. Howard, showing the true impatience of someone who has seen the possibility of political trans-formation, dates the arrival of the politics of the future to around 2020, when the internet of things will kick into gear. That's pretty much now.

Yet Howard recognises this as only one possibility. There are many others. The subtitle of his book is 'How the Internet of Things May Set Us Free or Lock Us Up'. Contained in the technology that has the power to liberate us are the worst-case scenarios, too, involving vast abuses of power, growing inequality and political paralysis. Putting our faith in the emancipatory potential of machines requires a huge leap of faith.

To get to the best possible future we have to run the gauntlet of the worst. Moreover, we have to start from where we are now. The present contains hints of times to come but it is dominated by the echoes of the past. The democracy that many have grown to dislike and distrust remains a comfortable and familiar place to be, compared with the prospect of the unknown. This is our mid-life crisis. We may prefer to wallow in it.

CONCLUSION

This is how democracy ends

ALL DEMOCRACIES – all societies – look to the fortunes of other states in the hope of glimpsing their own future. When a rival is on the march, we want to know if that means we are about to be eclipsed. When another democracy starts to fall apart, we want to know if it's a warning of our own possible fate. Democratic politics is hungry for morality tales, so long as it is someone else who is living them.

In the late 1980s many Western commentators viewed Japan as the coming power: the twenty-first century would be the Japanese century. Francis Fukuyama cited Japan (along with the EU) as the likeliest illustration of what we could expect from the end of history: the triumph of democracy would turn out to be stable, prosperous, efficient and just a little bit boring. Then the Japanese bubble burst – along with the Japanese stock market – and the future belonged to someone else. Japan became instead a fable about the dangers of hubris. As the country embarked on its lost decades of zero growth and political stagnation it offered a stark warning to others. Bubbles can burst anywhere.

By 2010 it was Greece that was flashing red. The EU was no longer boring – it was deeply alarming. Politicians across the Western world held up Greece as an example of what could happen if democracies did not get their debts under control. When he became UK Chancellor of the Exchequer in 2010, George Osborne used the Greek financial crisis as the ultimate morality tale. 'You can see in Greece the example of a country that didn't face up to its problems, and that is the fate I want to avoid,' he said, launching Britain on a decade-long programme of austerity.[91] Now that decade is almost up and Greece has lost much of its capacity to frighten the children. The country has not fallen into the abyss. Austerity has not made the difference that was promised. Life goes on.

Today Japan and Greece are rarely invoked by politicians in other democracies as exemplars of the possible fate that awaits us all. They don't work as morality tales any more because their message has grown too ambiguous. Japan remains stuck in a political and economic rut yet it continues to function perfectly well as a stable, affluent society that looks after its citizens. Imagine drawing a ticket in the great lottery of life that assigned a time and a place in which to live from across the sweep of human history. If it read: 'Japan, early twenty-first century', you would still feel like you'd won the jackpot. Greece is in more of a mess, yet it too remains prosperous and peaceful by historical standards. There are many, many grimmer places than this. The crisis was never resolved but the worst never happened either.

So we look for fresh instances of the coming thing. China has supplanted Japan as the Eastern giant that haunts the Western political imagination. China may be about to overtake us; alternatively, China could be where the next big bubble bursts. Venezuela has replaced Greece as the place whose miserable current fate serves as a warning against playing with the fire of populism. In his October 2017 Conservative Party conference speech, the UK Chancellor of the Exchequer Philip Hammond warned against 'Venezuelan-style' food shortages and violence on the streets if Jeremy Corbyn became prime minister. Any possible President or Prime Minister Leftist is liable to be held up as a Maduro in the making, just as any President or Prime Minister Rightist is painted as a potential Orban, or worse still a would-be Trump. We want our warnings to be clear-cut: there but for the grace of God goes democracy.

Yet ironically, it is Japan and Greece that now offer the best guides to how democracy might end up, long after politicians looking for a cheap hit have lost interest in them. Stable democracies retain their extraordinary capacity to stave off the worst that can happen without tackling the problems that threatened disaster in the first place. The Greek crisis has been kicked down the road so many times that we have to conclude the road is a lot longer than seemed possible. Who knows where it ends? As I write, the Greek economy is slowly starting to grow again for the first time in more than eight years. The debt burden is higher than ever. Prime Minister Tsipras is more unpopular than at any other point in his premiership. The party of the Greek centre right that presided over the first phase of the never-ending crisis may be on the brink of a return to power. Varoufakis has another book out.

Greece and Japan are very different places to live but they have some features in common. They are two of the oldest societies on the face of the earth: Japan is one of the very few countries with a higher proportion of elderly people in it than Greece. Half its population is aged 47 or older. Both nations desperately need an influx of youth. In the absence of a serious bump in the birth rate – and it is very hard to see what would trigger that – the obvious solution is immigration. Yet in both countries taking more immigrants – especially young men – is politically toxic and practically hard to manage. Eventually something will have to give. Perhaps if they wait long enough the robots will be able to do most of the work that young people used to, leaving the old to eke out their days playing computer games and worrying about their health. That could be how we all turn Japanese in the end. There are worse fates.

Japan is also one of the least violent societies on earth. Its murder rate is the lowest in the developed world. Japanese politics is still rife with scandal – accusations of bribery are never far from felling one politician or another – yet riots and street violence are almost unknown. Political conflict is venomous and toothless at the same time. Greece has higher crime levels than Japan but violence remains rare there, too, not just by historical standards but even in comparison with other places in Europe (the murder rate in Greece is lower than in the UK). Nearly a decade of brutal economic depression has done little to change that. Greece has fallen apart without falling apart. Its politics has turned vicious without turning violent. Some democracies, it seems, can absorb an awful lot of pain.

The stories of Japan and Greece turn out to be different from what might have been feared, or even from what might have been hoped. As morality tales go, they are missing something. What they lack is a moral. Instead of the drama reaching a climax, democracy persists in a kind of frozen crouch, holding on, waiting it out, even if it is far from clear what anyone is waiting for. After a while, the waiting becomes the point of the exercise. Something will turn up eventually. It always does.

This is not the whole story, of course. Many

democracies, even in the West, are less elderly than Japan and Greece, more volatile, more impatient, and potentially a lot more violent. One does not have to go to Caracas to get a glimpse of an alternative future. Chicago will do.

The claim that violence is in overall decline – most famously made by Steven Pinker in *The Better Angels of our Nature* (2011) – has underpinned some of my argument in this book.[92] That picture has grown more complicated in recent years. A significant part of Pinker's case was based on falling crime rates across the US, from their highs in the 1970s and 1980s down to historic lows in the 2010s. But the murder rate there has gone up by almost 10 per cent in the last two years, much of the increase coming from the toll in a few cities: Las Vegas, Baltimore and Chicago. On average more than fifty people a month are shot to death in Chicago. The toll there is much higher than it was even in the notoriously violent 1920s.

This recent rise in violence is very patchy. While some cities are experiencing dramatic spikes, others remain relatively untouched. In 2016 New York's crime rate was still at a record low. In Chicago, the violence leaves large parts of the city alone: out of more than seventy police districts, just five account for two-thirds of the increase in killing. It is possible to live right next to a bloodbath and yet to be more or less immune from it.

Chicago-style murder is not the most dramatic outbreak of violence currently sweeping the US. An even greater toll comes from self-harm. The suicide rate is up sharply this decade, notably in rural areas. More Americans currently shoot themselves than shoot others. The opioid epidemic now rampant across parts of America is taking far more lives than gun violence and shows no sign of stopping. Road deaths are also on the rise. As a result, the US is the first country in the developed world that has seen a decline in life expectancy. More than 100,000 Americans died last year either from an overdose or in a road accident. This is the true American carnage.

What the US is currently experiencing could be called the long tail of violence: there is plenty of it, but most of it is tailored to particular groups. It is rarely a collective experience. Violence has not disappeared. Instead, it has spread out and thinned out, touching individual lives in myriad ways that barely register with those not directly affected. Much of this violence is privatised, domesticated or institutionalised in places designed to keep it off the minds of the majority. The American prison system, in which more than two million people are incarcerated, including a vastly disproportionate number of young African-American men, is a giant factory of violence that deliberately takes it outside of politics. Out of sight, out of mind.

At the same time, the shadow of some unspeakably violent cataclysm hangs over the entire country. Certain individual acts of violence – especially when perpetrated by terrorists – get treated as harbingers of a general collapse. One false move and we could all be dead. Trump embodies this phenomenon. He deals in two kinds of political violence: the low-level, attritional variety that manifests in personal abuse; and the threat of nuclear Armageddon. In every long tail distribution, along with the proliferation of tiny events, there is a small number of overwhelming ones. Trump seems able to do almost nothing to reach out to the millions of Americans who are at risk from everyday violence. Yet he is quite capable of destroying millions himself.

The long tail of violence is emblematic of the bind democracy is in: the threats it faces are either too big or too small. What the opioid epidemic and the risk of nuclear war with North Korea have in common is the difficulty democratic politics finds in getting a grip on them. The space between the personal and the apocalyptic, which is where democratic politics traditionally plays out, has become a battleground for rival world views which are informed by personal or apocalyptic expectations of the worst that could happen. Mid-level politics is what's missing. In any long tail distribution, it is the middle that gets hit hardest.[93] Contemporary democracy is no exception. Macro events and micro experiences squeeze out the room for reasonable compromise. When people look for the institutions that might facilitate such compromise, they find that they have been hollowed out by the pull of political fears and frustrations that are either too big or too small to fit them.

Despite this, one reason democracy is able to cling on is that it retains its negative capabilities. Frustrations have their uses, however empty the spaces in which they rattle around. When people are thoroughly sick of some politicians they can still replace them with others. Terrible leaders – 'bad emperors', as they used to be called in China – can be dispatched relatively painlessly. Moribund political parties get carted off to the breakers' yard, eventually. A truly inattentive or cowed democracy may find that a bad emperor is able to worm himself into its institutions, making it hard to get rid of him. Erdogan has been around in Turkey for eighteen years now, and shows no sign of going away. But that will not happen with Trump. American democracy is neither cowed nor inattentive enough to allow him to stay in office beyond 2025. And he is very unlikely to last that long.

Democracies remain good at putting off the evil day. Their inability to get a grip or to keep a sense of perspective is useful for delaying the worst, even if it is deeply frustrating when it comes to trying to do much better than that. Kicking the can down the road is what democracies are best at. That's why the road may turn out to be longer than we thought.

The problem for twenty-first century democracy is that its positive virtues are coming apart. Simply staving off disaster is not enough. For democracy to flourish it needs to retain its ability to combine net benefits with personal recognition. That is not happening any more. There are still benefits and there is still recognition: they just don't go together. Solutions to our shared problems, which depend more and more on technical expertise, are moving one way, towards technocracy. Demands for recognition, which are increasingly expressed in the language of personal identity, are moving the other way, towards something close to anarchism. During the twentieth century the collective experience of political struggle – both to solve shared problems and to enhance democratic recognition – kept democracy intact. In the twenty-first century the dispersed experience of political anger is pulling it apart.

Political parties were once the primary instruments for combining democracy's positive virtues. Now these parties are being pulled apart, too, as the politics of personal recognition fuels frustration with the mechanics of democratic representation. Because this is democracy, no one wants to talk openly about how hard it has become. Politicians at election time still promise to be all things to all people: this social movement will solve your personal problems; that personality cult will make your country whole again. These empty promises catch up with the politicians before long, at which point they are replaced by other ones. But democracy does not get any better.

The digital revolution is accelerating this process. It is also emblematic of it. The most vociferous 'solvers' are often the tech titans, who believe that their machines have the capacity to tackle the world's intractable problems. These cult leaders of the new solutionism, along with their many devotees, have nothing against democracy because they are sure that anything which enhances our problem-solving ability is a democratic plus. At the same time, they remain confident that their technology is able to supply democratic recognition across the board: it is giving voice to the voiceless. What they cannot tell us is how these two things go together. Because they don't.

This makes Mark Zuckerberg a bigger threat to American democracy than Donald Trump. Zuckerberg has no evil designs on democratic institutions; indeed, he seems to have very little gripe with democracy at all. His intentions are good. That is the threat he poses. The central challenge democracy faces is to find a way to reconnect what has come apart, which means first of all seeing that simply pushing harder at the two sides of democratic life without connecting them will do no good. American democracy can survive Trump because its negative virtues will see him off. But its negative virtues are no help in seeing off Zuckerberg, because that would require something more positive. The institutions we need to confront the political emptiness we increasingly feel are the ones that supercharged solutionism and supercharged expressionism are hollowing out.

This is likely to be democracy's fate: the Trumps will come and go; the Zuckerbergs will keep going. Nothing too terrible is being threatened because Zuckerberg wants nothing terrible to happen. Plenty of problems will get solved, though plenty of new ones will be created, too. Many of the alienated will have a chance to find their voice. And slowly but surely, democracy will come to an end.

What is my solution? At this point in any book about the malaise of contemporary democracy there is usually an expectation that the author will suggest some fixes. I do not have any. If solutionism is part of the problem, simply proposing solutions is not going to be the way to fix it.

Instead, let me offer some lessons for the twenty-first century. These are not intended as a guide to the future. Rather, they are a way of understanding where we are now. No matter how we end up, we ought to know where we are starting from.

- Mature, Western democracy is over the hill. Its prime is past. We ought to acknowledge this: an extremely successful and dynamic form of politics, that enjoyed a remarkable hundred-year run, is winding down in the places where it has had its greatest successes. That still leaves room for plenty of meaningful choices. If the latter part of this story is to come, a lot could yet happen. The declining years of anyone's life are sometimes the most fulfilling. But that will only be the case if we can get out of the funk we are in at the moment, when we are spending too much time trying to recapture our lost youth.

- At the same time, we can't allow ourselves to become preoccupied with death. Democratic politics is being stifled by the intimations of mortality that it has begun to recognise. In many ways, we are right to be frightened: something terminal could be around the corner. Blithe confidence in the future would be ridiculous at this stage. We have a lot more to fear than fear itself. But we also have to recognise that, while democracy still has life left in it, it has to be lived. If the period till the end is spent worrying about the end, the time between will simply pass by in a blur.

- Death is not what it was. The unambiguous termination of a life has morphed into something more like an incremental process. This is true for individual human beings, who can be kept alive in some functions well after other essential features of life have ceased. Dementia can rob a person of her identity without impacting on her bodily integrity. Such a half-life can endure for a very long time. With the current pace of technological advances we should expect some half-lives to last longer than many full ones. The same will be true of our political systems. Democracy will almost certainly have a drawn-out demise. Artificial enhancements, delays and technical fixes can keep it on life support almost indefinitely. The strength of democracy remains its ability to disaggregate problems so that they become manageable. That means democracy should be able to disaggregate its own death. It can put it off, piece by piece.

- Democracy is not us. The demise of democracy is not our demise. Its salvation is not our salvation. The analogy between a human life and the life of a political system only goes so far. There is a danger that as democracy starts to wind down, we overcompensate in our attempts to keep it going. We could save democracy and destroy the world. There are no better alternatives around at present, but that does not mean that none are possible. If we keep insisting that democracy is sacrosanct

– in particular, if we think that ploughing on with election after election will spark it back into life – we will eventually lose sight of what we are trying to achieve. We will simply be going through the motions.

- The history of democracy will not have a single endpoint, unless all human life does. There will still be success stories, particularly in the places where democracy retains something of its youthful promise. There will also be outright disasters – some democracies are liable to collapse as they did in the past. As I write this, Brazilian democracy appears particularly vulnerable. Nearly half of all Brazilians in a recent poll expressed support for the idea of a 'temporary military intervention'[94] to address the country's current economic and political crisis. Coups will still happen, though given the multitude ways democracy can be used as cover for its own gradual erosion, they will become increasingly rare. But mature Western democracies need to stop looking for other states to tell them what's coming: Brazil is not the new Greece. We can't live vicariously, any more than we can die vicariously. We have to go through this ourselves.

Western democracy will survive its mid-life crisis. With luck, it will be a little chastened by it. It is unlikely to be revived by it. This is not, after all, the end of democracy. But this is how democracy ends.

EPILOGUE

20 January 2053

IS THERE ANYTHING we can know for sure about what's coming in the second half of the twenty-first century? The twenty-year horizon of technological transformation, however long delayed, makes everything beyond seem extremely hazy. It is almost impossible to imagine what everyday life might be like if the line between human and machine intelligence gets crossed; never mind what politics might be like. Even if we don't cross that line, the pace of change is unlikely to slow. Prediction is a hazardous business at the best of times. In the digital age, it is a fool's errand.

Yuval Noah Harari has argued that the digital revolution marks the true end of history, because it spells the demise of human agency as the primary determinant of social change. We can't imagine what will happen in the remainder of this century because we suspect it doesn't really depend on us. It will be shaped for us by machines, which will render many of the basic categories of human existence obsolete. Harari believes that individuality, conscience, moral judgement and democratic choice will all become remnants of the historical past. That is what makes the future unknowable for the people we are now. Progress will be measured by the efficient use of information. Human experience will be reduced to a series of data points.[95]

Maybe. But to arrive at any dystopia, we still have to get from here to there. The question remains of what happens in between. Our worst nightmares are always liable to be blocked by the obstacles that the remnants of history put in their way. Few social phenomena end with a bang. Most have a long half-life. Democracy is no exception.

I will make this prediction: on 20 January 2053 there will be a ceremony in Washington DC to mark the inauguration of the duly elected president of the United States. Few if any other dates in the calendar of the future have such a degree of certainty attached. Americans have inaugurated a president at the height of a terrible civil war, in the midst of two world wars and in the depths of a catastrophic economic depression. It will take more than the digital revolution to derail this event. The world would have to be coming to an end.

American democracy will survive the presidency of Donald Trump. Barring utter catastrophe, there will be no coup and there will be no collapse in the rule of law. Democratic politics will limp on. History will continue. The political future is unknowable but a generation from now it will still be recognisable as a relic of the past.

MONDAY, 20 JANUARY 2053 was another lovely day in Washington. It was sufficiently warm that few on the platform had need of coats and scarves. January was now recognised as the best month to be in the city – a brief period of respite before the rains arrived.

The new president looked confident and relaxed. He had been elected with just 28 per cent of the popular vote, the smallest total for a winning candidate in history. Nevertheless, it had been a comfortable victory. None of his six main rivals had got within ten points of him. The reformed Electoral College, which gave him a bonus for winning the popular vote, had helped. But he had won enough of the unreformed, winner-take-all states to get him over the line with such a paltry vote share anyway.

President Li, as was by now traditional, had won by running at the head of his own personal movement against the established political parties. His message had been simple: he would take on the power of the giant tech corporations. Both the Democrats and the Republicans had fielded two candidates each, having once again been unable to agree on a procedure to arrive at one who was acceptable to the entire party. The two parties looked finished, though people had been saying that for years. Li had also seen off the solar power magnate who had bankrolled her own campaign and the crowd-funded pop star who came a distant second. The final presidential debate, which had turned into a free-for-all, had done no one any favours.

Everyone could agree that presidential politics were a mess. The long-running campaign to reform the American electoral system to include two rounds of voting – on the model of the now-defunct French Fifth Republic – had come to nothing. Though many voters were nostalgic for the days when presidential elections had offered a binary choice, it had proved impossible to secure agreement to change the constitution. They were stuck with what they'd got.

Some states had gone back to insisting on paper ballots, after the scandal of the 'e-election' eight years earlier, which had taken two years to resolve in the courts. Eventually, President Chan-Zuckerberg had been permitted to remain in office on the understanding that state rights over vote counting were restored. California had chosen to stick with the facial recognition system that had caused all the trouble in the first place. In Minnesota, voters now had to attend their polling places in person and to prove their identity by showing their DNA samples.

President Li's arrival in office had been dogged by rumours that he was in the pocket of the Chinese government. These accusations did him little harm. Most voters had long since learned to disregard stories of this kind. Anyway, for plenty of them, having a president with Chinese ties was a plus, given how many Chinese connections they had of their own. Li had also survived a minor scandal when it emerged that as a young man he had been employed for a short time by Facebook, before leaving to set up his own business. He argued that if you were going to tame the beast you needed to understand how it worked from the inside. This was a lie. Li had only ever been an accountant in the finance division. He had no real idea how the business worked.

Li had encouraged his supporters to go offline in the weeks before the presidential vote, so that the result wouldn't be known in advance. His strategy worked and millions heeded his advice. 'Vote, don't share!' became a winning campaign slogan. But the result of the election came as no surprise to anyone – the dramatic drop in network activity had made it clear that Li would win, and it also revealed who exactly was planning to vote for him. When they went back online the day after the vote, his supporters were greeted with messages of congratulations from their host servers.

The central plank of Li's campaign had been his defence of the beleaguered dollar, which he called 'the people's money'. He had promised to start printing banknotes again for spending within the borders of the

United States. This was popular with the victims of the great block-chain deflation, including many indebted college graduates who had long since given up trying to find a permanent job.

Li's coalition was made up of the stay-at-homes, who lived off their meagre universal basic income, and the travellers, who moved from state to state looking for part-time work. His support was lowest among the over-80s, who were worried he would substitute their retirement income with dollars. The old had grown attached to their Bitcoins. They needn't have feared – during the transition the Chair of the Federal Reserve had already explained to the President-Elect that it would be impossible to make paper money forgery-proof. Li had been forced to drop the idea. He was still looking for another one.

There was little expectation that Li would be able to get much done, given the Congress that had been elected with him. The divided parties, and the increasing number of independents winning office, had further fractured the political landscape. The elaborate checks and balances of the American constitution, still intact, made it far easier for the legislature to prevent law-making than to accomplish it. Libertarians welcomed this development. The many others who regretted it could see no way round the basic problem – a constitution that provided so many opportunities for veto had placed a veto in the way of its own reform. In the past, a national emergency might have removed some of these barriers. But by now the political landscape was too fractured for one of those either.

Not all of Li's rivals came to his inauguration. Three stayed away, claiming that his election on such a paltry vote share was nothing but an empty charade. It made little difference. The occasion was well attended by an enthusiastic crowd and any protests were kept to a minimum. The joint chiefs were there, along with various congressional leaders and members of the Supreme Court. All was as it should be. The ceremony passed without a hitch.

Li was not in possession of the nuclear codes, but no president had been given those in thirty years, ever since Congress had devolved the ultimate decision about the use of America's nuclear arsenal to a committee of three, consisting of the Head of the Joint Chiefs, the Speaker of the House and a White House nominee, who was by convention the President's Chief of Staff. These three were connected at all times by their own private network and no decision could be taken without their joint agreement. They soon became known as 'the three wise men', not without irony, given how many times America had come to the brink of nuclear war since then. Now, for the first time, all three would be women.

Li's inaugural address was short and stirring. The stage was draped with real American flags, not the virtual ones that had fluttered in previous years. He spoke of his election as the moment when power would be returned from the owners of the world's social networks to the people's representatives in Washington DC. Decisions that affected all Americans would be taken in the interests of all Americans. He reminded his audience that the United States of America was, first and foremost, still a democracy. It always would be a democracy.

As he left the stage, his immediate predecessor but one was heard to remark to her neighbour: 'He protests too much.'

Further reading

I HAVE BEEN THINKING about the theme of how much trouble democracy is in for quite a while. Plenty of other people have been thinking and writing about this theme, too. In addition to the books and articles I refer to in the text, there are lots worth reading on this topic. Here are some that have helped inform my own thinking. I don't agree with all of them, and this book is often trying to say something different. But they are all full of insight and interest.

On the big questions that have preoccupied contemporary political scientists – what causes democracy to stick and what causes it to slide backwards – one very influential answer is given by Daron Acemoglu and James Robinson in *Why Nations Fail: The Origins of Power, Prosperity, and Poverty* (New York: Crown Business, 2012; London: Profile, 2013). They identify trustworthy institutions as the key to political stability. This is a more accessible version of their classic earlier book, *The Economic Origins of Dictatorship and Democracy* (Cambridge: Cambridge University Press, 2005). The initial book has some equations in it; the later one doesn't.

Francis Fukuyama, still best known for *The End of History and the Last Man* (New York and London: Free Press, 1992), gives his own account of the rise and possible fall of democracy in *The Origins of Political Order* (New York: Farrer, Straus & Giroux; London: Profile, 2012) and *Political Order and Political Decay* (New York: Farrer, Straus & Giroux, 2014; London: Profile, 2015). The second volume in particular, with its concerns about the inflexibility of American 'vetocracy', should dispel any lingering illusions that Fukuyama is a blithe optimist.

Steven Levitsky and Daniel Ziblatt's *How Democracies Die: What History Tells Us about Our Future* (New York: Crown; London: Viking, 2018) was published too late for me to address its arguments in this book. It takes a different line than I do, by using the history of democratic failure to provide a guide to how and why American democracy might go wrong in the present and future. It is the most up-to-date account we have of what causes democratic 'backsliding' and how to evaluate Trump on that scale. I hope my book, with its similar but very different title, complements rather than contradicts theirs.

The Journal of Democracy has published many compelling articles in recent years on the question of where the current weaknesses of democracy lie. Some are fairly gloomy. In addition to the one on coups by Nancy Bermeo that I discuss in this book, two very influential articles are 'The Democratic Disconnect' (July 2016) and 'The Signs of Deconsolidation' (January 2017) by Yascha Mounk and Robert Stefan Foa. They highlight polling and other evidence that suggests the attachment to democratic values in the established democracies may be waning, especially among young people.

There are many excellent books on what went wrong for democracy in the 1930s. Richard J. Evans, who now sees some parallels between the failure of democracy in the Weimar period and the rise of Donald Trump, tells the original story in *The Coming of the Third Reich* (New York: The Penguin Press, 2004; London: Allen Lane, 2003). The most compelling account of how close American democracy came to disaster in the 1930s, and the compromises by which disaster was avoided, is Ira Katznelson's *Fear Itself: The New Deal and the Origins of Our Time* (New York and London: Liveright, 2014).

Going further back, Paul Cartledge's *Democracy: A Life* (New York and Oxford: Oxford University Press, 2012, 2016) brings ancient Athenian politics alive for the present, in all its complexity and strangeness. A very different sort of book is *Democracy: A Case Study* by David A. Moss (Cambridge, MA: Belknap Press, 2017). This evaluates episodes in the history of American democracy – its successes and its failures – according to the score sheet of the Harvard Business School. It is not an approach that will be to everyone's tastes, but it does bring out how extensions to the franchise have been instrumental in getting democracy out of its periodic ruts, and how hard that might be to achieve today.

In contemporary political theory, Nadia Urbinati's *Democracy Disfigured: Opinion, Truth, and the People* (Cambridge, MA: Harvard University Press, 2014) does a masterly job of unpicking the different ways that contemporary democracy can turn the people into spectators. Along with her previous book, *Representative Democracy: Principles & Genealogy* (Chicago: University of Chicago Press, 2006), which characterises democracy as the politics of 'second thoughts', this work has had a deep influence on how I understand modern politics.

A growing number of recent books take the phenomenon of conspiracy theories seriously. One of the earliest, and still one of the best, is Kathryn Olmsted's *Real Enemies: Conspiracy Theories and American*

Democracy, World War I to 9/11 (New York: Oxford University Press, 2009). Pankaj Mishra's *Age of Anger: A History of the Present* (New York: Farrer, Straus & Giroux; London: Allen Lane, 2017) tells a long story of popular political anger that runs from Jean-Jacques Rousseau to the current assault on elites around the world. In doing so Mishra joins the dots from nineteenth-century Italian nationalism to Trump and Modi. Jan-Werner Muller's *What is Populism?* (Philadelphia, PA: University of Pennsylvania Press, 2016; London: Penguin Books, 2017) is a short and pithy account of what makes contemporary populism a distinctive form of politics.

The book that helped to kick-start the existential risk industry was Martin Rees's *Our Final Century? Will the Human Race Survive the Twenty-first Century?* (London: William Heinemann, 2003). In paperback it was published without the first question mark. Nick Bostrom's *Superintelligence: Paths, Dangers, Strategies* (Oxford: Oxford University Press, 2014) has highlighted the potentially catastrophic risks of AI for a wide audience, including in Silicon Valley. Sonia (S. M.) Amadae's *Prisoners of Reason: Game Theory and Neoliberal Political Economy* (Cambridge: Cambridge University Press, 2016) makes the connection between nuclear war, game theory and contemporary economics. She shows that some kinds of existential risk are nothing new.

For more on the complex history of the relationship between states and corporations – and the hybrid models that have existed between them – a timely study is *International Order in Diversity: War, Trade and Rule in the Indian Ocean* by Andrew Philips and J. C. Sharman (Cambridge: Cambridge University Press, 2015). The authors believe that the hegemony of the sovereign state is the exception even in relatively recent history, not the rule. They may well be right.

There is now a proliferation of books trying to dissect what digital technology means for the functioning of democracy. Frank Pasquale's *The Black Box Society: The Secret Algorithms That Control Money and Information* (Cambridge, MA: Harvard University Press, 2015) explains why having algorithms decide things for us will be bad for democracy. On the positive side of the ledger, Geoff Mulgan's *Big Mind: How Collective Intelligence Can Change Our World* (Princeton, NJ: Princeton University Press, 2017) explores the problem-solving potential of machine learning for democracy. In *Political Turbulence: How Social Media Shape Collective Action* (Princeton, NJ: Princeton University Press, 2015), Helen Margetts and her co-authors dispel some illusions about echo chambers and the prevalence of groupthink online. As always, the real story is both better and worse than we might imagine.

In this book I reference novels as well as works of non-fiction. One that I don't discuss is Philip Roth's *The Plot Against America* (Boston: Houghton Mifflin; London: Jonathan Cape, 2004). In many ways it goes against the themes I am trying to pursue, because Roth imagines an alternative America of the early 1940s, where a fascist manages to make it all the way to the White House. Roth wants us to reflect on how what didn't happen once could none the less happen again. He was writing more than a decade before Trump, in the time of George W. Bush and the Patriot Act. Even in the age of Trump, I don't think Roth's alternative past is our collective future. Still, it is one of the scariest and most compelling works of fiction I have ever read.

Acknowledgements

Some of the thinking behind this book comes out of two collaborative research projects I have been involved with in Cambridge: Conspiracy and Democracy (http://www .conspiracyanddemocracy.org) and Technology and Democracy (http://www.techdem.crassh.cam.ac.uk). I am very grateful to my colleagues on these projects for their stimulation and support. I owe a particular debt of gratitude to John Naughton, who has worked with me on both, and has been a tireless source of encouragement and ideas. I couldn't have written this book without his help.

I am also very grateful to the guests and colleagues who have taken part with me on the Talking Politics podcast (https://www.talkingpoliticspodcast.com). We have spent a lot of time over the past eighteen months talking about the state of democracy and I learn something every time we do. I particularly want to thank Helen Thompson: she is the person from whom I have learnt most of all.

Andrew Franklin at Profile Books suggested that I write this book and he has been a model editor to work with: friendly but expectant. So, too, has Lara Heimert at Basic Books. I offer them and others at both publishers my thanks for their hard work and enthusiasm. My agent, Peter Straus, has also been a great champion of this book. I received invaluable research assistance from Benjamin Studebaker, who discussed some of the ideas in this book with me and gave me some new ones.

An early outline of the argument of this book came in an article I wrote in the *London Review of Books* called 'Is This How Democracy Ends?', which appeared in the immediate aftermath of Trump's victory, in December 2016. I am grateful as always to Mary-Kay Wilmers and the editorial staff at the *LRB* for all they do to support my writing.

Finally, my deepest thanks and love go to my wife Bee Wilson and our children Tom, Natasha and Leo. Bee was writing a book of her own at the same time as I was writing mine. The fact that I finished first reflects far better on her than it does on me.

Notes

Preface

1   Francis Fukuyama, 'The End of History?', *The National Interest*, Summer 1989 (16), pp. 3–18.

Introduction

2   'The Inaugural Address', *The White House, The United States Government*, 20 January 2017, http://bit.ly/2mLGtmv

3   This idea originates with Adam Przeworski, 'Minimalist conception of democracy: a defense', in *Democracy's Value*, Ian Shapiro & Casiano Hacker Cordon, eds. (Cambridge: Cambridge University Press, 1999)

4   'Statement by the President', *National Archives and Records Administration*, 9 November 2016, http://bit.ly/2A28UVs

5   As above.

6   'What we are in the middle of and what we have been in the middle of, essentially since election night and all the days following, is a silent coup', *The Rush Limbaugh Show*, 12 July 2017, http://bit.ly/2hU1lLW

1   Coup!

7   C. L. Sulzberger, 'Greece under the Colonels', *Foreign Affairs*, vol. 48, no. 2, 1970, http://fam.ag/2zjK029

8   As above.

9   Yanis Varoufakis, *Adults in the Room: My Battle With Europe's Deep Establishment* (London: The Bodley Head, 2017), p. 78.

10 As above, p. 469.

11 As above, p. 82.

12 Donald Kagan, *Studies in the Greek Historians* (Cambridge: Cambridge University Press, 2009), p. 46.

13 Edward N. Luttwak, *Coup D'État: A Practical Handbook* (Harmondsworth: Penguin Books, 1968), p. 9.

14 As above, p. 24.

15 Quoted in Adam Roberts, 'Civil resistance to military coups', *Journal of Peace Research* (12, 1975), p. 26.

16 Jonathan Fenby, *The General: Charles De Gaulle and the France He Saved* (London: Simon & Schuster, 2010), p. 467.

17 Nancy Bermeo, 'On democratic backsliding', *Journal of Democracy*, (27, 2016), pp. 5–19.

18 As above, p. 14.

19 Bruce Ackerman, *The Decline and Fall of the American Republic* (Cambridge, MA: Harvard University Press, 2010).

20 Sam Bourne, *To Kill the President* (London: HarperCollins, 2017).

21 Chris Mullin, *A Very British Coup* (London: Hodder & Stoughton, 1982).

22 Joseph E. Uscinski et al., 'Conspiracy theories are for losers', *APSA 2011 Annual Meeting Paper*, August 2011 http://bit.ly/2zr6OBx

23 Joseph E. Uscinski & Joseph M. Parent, *American Conspiracy Theories* (New York: Oxford University Press, 2014).

24 *See* Joel Rogers, 'Are conspiracy theories for (political) losers?', YouGov–Cambridge, 13 February 2015, http://bit.ly/2ACrfI5 (full survey results: http://bit.ly/2k2kvNf).

25 Quoted in Christian Davies, 'The conspiracy theorists who have taken over Poland,' *Guardian* 'Long Read', 16 February 2016 http://bit.ly/2enJyVI

26 *See* 'Free silver and the mind of "Coin" Harvey', in Richard Hofstadter, *The Paranoid Style in American Politics* (New York: Vintage, 2008).

27 For the classic version of this story, see Richard Hofstadter, *The Age of Reform: From Bryan to F.D.R.* (New York: Alfred A. Knopf, 1955).

28 Thomas Piketty, *Capital in the Twenty-first Century* (Cambridge, MA: Harvard University Press, 2014).

29 Walter Scheidel, *The Great Leveler: Violence and the History of Inequality From the Stone Age to the Twenty-first Century* (Princeton, NJ: Princeton University Press, 2017).

2 Catastrophe!

30 Rachel Carson, 'Silent spring – I', *New Yorker*, 16 June 1962, http://bit.ly/2zYoOlx

31 John Hersey, 'Hiroshima', *New Yorker,* 31 August 1946, http://bit.ly/2yibwPT

32 Hannah Arendt, 'Eichmann in Jerusalem – I', *New Yorker*, 16 February1963 (and four following issues), http://bit.ly/2gkvNOi

33 As above.

34 'The desolate year', *Monsanto Magazine*, October 1962, pp. 4–9.

35 Paul Krugman, 'Pollution and politics', *New York Times*, 27 November 2014, http://nyti.ms/2B288H9

36 Eben Harrell, 'The four horsemen of the nuclear apocalypse', *Time*, 10 March 2011, http://ti.me/2hMn8RY

37 Timothy Snyder, *On Tyranny: Twenty Lessons from the Twentieth Century* (London: The Bodley Head, 2017), p. 50.

38 Timothy Snyder, *Bloodlands: Europe Between Hitler and Stalin* (New York: Basic Books, 2010).

39 Derek Parfit, *Reasons and Persons* (Oxford: Oxford University Press, 1984), pp. 453ff.

40 Quoted in Craig Lambert, 'Nuclear weapons or democracy', *Harvard Magazine*, March 2014, http://bit.ly/2i2BFgc

41 Nick Bostrom, 'Existential risks: analyzing human extinction scenarios and related hazards', *Journal of Evolution and Technology* (9, 2002), http://bit.ly/2jSajtw

42 As above.

43 Raffi Khatchadourian, 'The Doomsday Invention', *New Yorker*, 23 November 2015, http://bit.ly/2zdfTJY

44 Cormac McCarthy, *The Road*, p. 54 (London: Picador, 2006).

45 David Mitchell, *The Bone Clocks* (London: Sceptre, 2014).

46 E. M. Forster, 'The Machine Stops' in *The Eternal Moment and Other Stories* (London: Sidgwick & Jackson, 1928).

47 Christopher Clark, *The Sleepwalkers: How Europe Went to War in 1914* (London: Allen Lane, 2013).

3   Technological takeover!

48 Mahatma Gandhi, *Hind Swaraj and Other Writings*, Anthony J. Parel, ed. (Cambridge: Cambridge University Press, 1997), p. 35.

49 David Edgerton, *Shock of the Old: Technology and Global History since 1900* (London: Profile, 2006).

50 Thomas Hobbes, *Leviathan*, Richard Tuck, ed. (Cambridge: Cambridge University Press, 1996), p. 9.

51 Mark Zuckerberg, 'Building global community', *Facebook*, 16 February 2017, http://bit.ly/2m39az5

52 Dave Eggers, *The Circle* (New York: Alfred A. Knopf, 2013).

53 Mark Zuckerberg, 'Mark Zuckerberg', *Facebook*, 3 January 2017, http://bit.ly/2hXwZIi

54 Josh Glancy, 'Mark Zuckerberg's "Listening Tour"', *Sunday Times*, 23 July 2017, http://bit.ly/2hVF4gM

55 Eggers, *The Circle*, p. 386.

56 The fullest account of this story is in Jon Ronson, *So You've Been Publicly Shamed* (New York: Riverhead Books, 2015).

57 Ezra Klein & Alvin Chang, '"Political identity is fair game for hatred": how Republicans and Democrats discriminate', *Vox*, 7 December 2015, http://bit. ly/2ja3CQb

58 'Mark Lilla vs identity politics', *The American Conservative*, 16 August 2017, http://bit.ly/2uTZYhy

59 '5th Republican debate transcript', *Washington Post*, 15 December 2015, http://wapo.st/2mTDrBY

60 Joseph Schumpeter, *Capitalism, Socialism, and Democracy* (New York: Harper and Brothers, 1942).

61 Joe McGinnis, *The Selling of the President 1968* (New York: Trident Press, 1969).

62 Robert A. Burton, 'Donald Trump, our AI president', *New York Times*, 22 May 2017, http://nyti.ms/2B3Rt6e

63 Quoted in L. A. Scaff, *Max Weber in America* (Princeton, NJ: Princeton University Press), p. 177.

4   Something better?

64 Nick Land, 'The Dark Enlightenment: part 1', *The Dark Enlightenment* (2013), http://bit.ly/2zZA5Cz

65 As above.

66 Curtis Yarvin, 'Moldbug's gentle introduction', *The Dark Enlightenment* (2009), http://bit.ly/2zft6lk

67 Alessio Piergiacomi, 'What would an AI government look like?' *Quora*, 30 April 2016.

68 As above.

69 Winston Churchill, House of Commons, 11 November 1947, http://bit.ly/2hMe3bR

70 Steven Levitsky & Lucan A. Way, *Competitive Authoritarianism: Hybrid Regimes after the Cold War* (Cambridge: Cambridge University Press, 2010).

71 Daniel A. Bell et al., 'Is the China model better than democracy?', *Foreign Policy*, 19 October 2015, http://atfp.co/1jRIJXC

72 As above.

73 John Stuart Mill, *Considerations on Representative Government* (London: Parker & Son, 1861).

74 Jason Brennan, *Against Democracy* (Princeton, NJ: Princeton University Press, 2016), p. 221.

75 As above, p. 212.

76 Christopher H. Achen & Larry M. Bartels, *Democracy for Realists: Why Elections Do Not Produce Responsive Government* (Princeton, NJ: Princeton University Press, 2016), p. 310.

77 Brennan, *Against Democracy*, p. 7.

78 David Estlund, *Democratic Authority: A Philosophical Framework* (Princeton, NJ: Princeton University Press, 2007).

79 Brennan, *Against Democracy*, p. 221.

80 Brian Wheeler, 'Nigel: the robot who could tell you how to vote,' *BBC News*, 17 September 2017, http://bbc.in/2x6K1IV

81 Benjamin M. Friedman, *The Moral Consequences of Economic Growth* (New York: Alfred A. Knopf, 2005).

82 Robert Nozick, *Anarchy, State, and Utopia* (New York: Basic Books, 1974), p. 310.

83 Paul Mason, *Postcapitalism: A Guide to Our Future* (London: Allen Lane, 2015).

84 As above, p. 134.

85 Philip N. Howard, *Pax Technica: How the Internet of Things May Set Us Free or Lock Us Up* (New Haven, CT: Yale University Press, 2015), p. 224.

86 As above, pp. 161–2.

87 Mason, *Postcapitalism*, p. 283.

88 Alex Williams & Nick Srnicek, '#ACCELERATE MANIFESTO for an accelerationist politics', *Critical Legal Thinking*, 14 May 2013, http://bit.ly/18usvb4

89 Yuval Noah Harari, *Homo Deus: A Brief History of Tomorrow* (London: Harvill Secker, 2016).

90 Derek Parfit, *Reasons and Persons* (Oxford: Oxford University Press, 1984), part 3.

Conclusion

91 'UK to dodge Greek fate with tough budget – Osborne', *Reuters*, 20 June 2010, http://reut.rs/2jSSnyZ

92 Steven Pinker, *The Better Angels of Our Nature: The Decline of Violence in History and Its Causes* (London: Allen Lane, 2011).

93 *See* Clay Shirky, 'Power laws, weblogs and inequality', 8 February 2003, http://bit.ly/1nyyc36

94 Alex Cuadros, 'Open talk of a military coup unsettles Brazil', *New Yorker*, 13 October 2017, http://bit.ly/2gjbW25

Epilogue

95 *See* Yuval, *Homo Deus*.

Index

Brennan, Jason: *Against Democracy*, 183–5, 186–7, 188–9
Bryan, William Jennings, 68–9
bureaucracies, 85, 86–7, 99, 127, 164; *see also* civil service
Burton, Robert, 159–60
Bush, President George W., 12, 55

C

Cambridge Analytica (firm), 156, 157, 159
capitalism, 196, 199
Carson, Rachel, 85, 87–8
Silent Spring, 82–3, 89, 90–91, 93
catastrophes, 6, 7, 85–6
environmental, 82–3, 85, 87–93; *see also* climate change
nuclear, 83–4, 97
total, 100
Chicago: violence, 211
China
and climate change, 174
Communist Party, 172–3
economy, 172, 208
foreign policy, 30–31
government model, 174
as a meritocracy, 175–6
nationalism, 172
pollution, 89
view of Trump, 173
Churchill, Winston, 8, 75–6, 168–9, 177
civil service, 41, 55–6; *see also* bureaucracies

Clark, Christopher: *The Sleepwalkers: How Europe Went to War in 1914*, 115
Clemenceau, Georges, 71, 75–6
climate change, 90–93
China and, 174
consciousness raising, 89, 92–93
conspiracy theories, 91–92
incremental nature of, 97
and risk, 101
support for, 108
and uncertainty, 96
see also global warming
Clinton, President Bill, 54–5
Clinton, Hillary, 13–15, 16, 198
Cold War, 28–9, 67, 94, 95–6, 106–7, 108–9
communism 194; *see also* China: Communist Party; Marxism-Leninism; Stalinism
consciousness raising, 85, 89, 92–3, 106
conspiracy theories, 60–71
climate change, 91–2
and division, 99
and fake news, 75
France, 69
India, 65–6
nuclear weapons, 96
Poland, 65, 66
and totalitarianism, 98
Turkey, 65, 66
United Kingdom, 62–3
United States, 62, 64–5, 67
and war, 77
conspiracy theorists, 153
Constantine I, King of Greece, 27, 28

G

game theory, 109–10
Gandhi, Mahatma, 120–22, 127, 131, 143, 145, 194
Hind Swaraj manifesto, 120–1
Garton Ash, Timothy, 176
Germany, 50
corporations, 130
election of Hitler, 18–19
and Greek debt, 32, 116–17
Weimar, 85, 97, 98, 99
global warming, 90, 102; *see also* climate change
Goldman, Emma, 194
Google, 131, 132–3, 136, 137, 139
Gore, Al, 120
Greece, 26–40, 50, 209–11
army, 30
Centre Union Party, 27
Cold War, 28–9
coups, 26–30, 32, 33, 34–5, 38, 40, 45
demography, 31–2
divisions, 29
economy, 31, 32–4, 39, 116–17, 176–7, 207–8, 209
elections, 28, 29, 39, 40, 148
foreign interest in, 30
Golden Dawn party, 30, 32
immigration, 210
National Radical Union (ERE), 28
news sources, 34–5
refugees, 30
Syriza government, 32, 39
technocracy, 181

violence, 28, 31, 210
see also Athens, ancient
Greece, ancient, 86; *see also* Athens, ancient
Grillo, Beppe, 162
Gulen, Fethullah, 52, 53

H

Hammond, Philip, 209
Hamon, Benoît, 148
Harari, Yuval Noah, 200, 219
Hersey, John: *Hiroshima*, 83–4, 85, 93–4
hierarchies, 137–9
Hitler, Adolf, 19, 99
Hobbes, Thomas, 130
Leviathan, 128–9, 133–4, 135, 151, 203–4
Hofstadter, Richard, 67
Howard, Philip N.: *Pax Technica*, 197–8, 205–6
Hungary, 175

I

Iceland, 162, 163
identity politics, 72, 150, 178, 202–3
immigration, 55, 68, 183, 184, 210
India
conspiracy theories, 65–6
independence, 120, 121
movement politics, 149
political enfranchisement, 76
pollution, 89
reform, 77
technology, 121–2
inequality
and corporations, 131

M

McCarthy, Cormac: *The Road*, 113, 118–19

McGinnis, Joe: *The Selling of the President*, 158

machines, 121–2, 125–6, 127, 196, 197, 199, 200–201, 202, 205, 219; *see also* artificial intelligence; computers; robots; technocracy; technology

McKinley, President William, 74

Macron, President Emanuel, 148, 149–50

Man on Wire (film), 117–18

Marx, Karl: 'The Fragment on Machines', 196–7

Marxism-Leninism, 171

Mason, Paul: *Postcapitalism*, 196, 197, 199, 205

Mélenchon, Jean-Luc, 58

Mencius Moldbug *see* Yarvin, Curtis

metadata, 154

Mill, John Stuart, 182–3, 185

Miller, Stephen, 13

mindlessness, 84, 86–8

Mitchell, David: *The Bone Clocks*, 113

Modi, Narendra, 65–6, 149

monarchs, 167

Monsanto (company): 'The Desolate Year', 88

Mugabe, President Robert, 48

Mullin, Chris: *A Very British Coup*, 58

N

NATO, 59

Nazis, 85, 97, 99

Netherlands, 148

networks
and anarchism, 193
and change, 196
interconnectedness, 112–15
political movements, 149
social 136, 151, 160, 177;
see also Facebook; social media; Twitter
utopian, 200
see also internet

New York
crime, 211
World Trade Center, 117–18

New York Times, 159–60

New Yorker (magazine), 82–3, 84, 106

news, fake, 64, 75, 98, 156, 157

Nixon, President Richard, 56, 90, 158

North Korea, 213

Nozick, Robert: *Anarchy, State, and Utopia*, 193–4, 195

nuclear disarmament, 107
Campaign for Nuclear Disarmament (CND), 94–5

nuclear weapons, 56, 83–4, 86, 94, 95, 96–7, 102, 103–104, 106, 107

Nunn, Sam, 95

O

Obama, President Barack
and climate change, 92
and conspiracy theory, 64

executive initiatives, 55
and inequality, 79
and Trump's election, 13, 14, 15, 16, 18
oil companies, 131
Orban, Viktor, 175
Osborne, George, 208
Oxford and Cambridge Review, 120

P

Papademos, Lucas, 39
Papandreou, Andreas, 27
Papandreou, George, 39
paranoia, 67, 74
Parent, Joe, 62
Parfit, Derek, 100, 202–3
Paul, Rand, 154
Perry, William, 95
pesticides, 87–9
Petit, Philippe, 117–18
Piergiacomi, Alessio, 167–8
Piketty, Thomas: *Capital in the Twenty-First Century*, 78
Pinker, Steven: *The Better Angels of our Nature*, 211
Plato, 179
Poland, 65, 66
police, 171
political parties, 214
    artificiality, 145–6
    charisma, 147
    and identity politics, 150
    as machines, 127
    membership, 146, 147–8
    'Net', 162
    partisan nature, 146
    'Pirate', 162
    United States, 146–7, 221

politicians: and trust, 144–5, 164, 214
pollution, 89, 90
populism, 13, 175
    and banality, 98–9
    causes of, 67
    and conspiracy theory, 65–7, 72, 168
    and disconnect, 141
    and economic growth, 192
    and inequality, 77–8
    and movement politics, 148–9
    United States, 67–70, 73
    and war, 75
precautionary principle, 100–101
pressure groups, 89
prisons, 151, 152, 212
Putin, President Vladimir, 157

R

racism, 143
Rand, Ayn, 194
rational choice theory, 108–9
referendums, 47–8, 179, 183
    France, 70
    Turkey, 52
    United Kingdom, 48
reform, 70, 71, 78, 79, 185;
    see also social change
revolutions, 41, 78, 196;
    see also digital revolution
risk, 101–5, 110–12, 116
robots, 7, 103, 111, 128–9, 130, 168, 210
Rockefeller, John D., 131–2
Roosevelt, President Theodore, 70, 71, 131

David Runciman is a professor of politics at Cambridge University. The author of five previous books and a contributing editor to the London Review of Books, he hosts the widely-acclaimed podcast "Talking Politics.' Runciman lives in Cambridge, United Kingdom.